Teaching dbook

Related Titles

Janet Kay: *Good Practice in Childcare*
Janet Kay: *Protecting Children*
Rosalind Millam: *Anti-discriminatory Practice*, second edition
Carole Sharman, Wendy Cross and Diana Vennis: *Observing Children*, second edition

Teaching Assistant's Handbook

Janet Kay

continuum
LONDON • NEW YORK

Continuum

The Tower Building
11 York Road
London SE1 7NX

370 Lexington Avenue
New York
NY 10017-6503

www.continuumbooks.com

First published 2002

British Library Cataloguing-in-Publication Data
A catalogue record for this book is available from the British Library.

ISBN: 0-8264-5498-4 (hardback)
      0-8264-5499-2 (paperback)

Typeset by YHT Ltd, London
Printed and bound in Great Britain by MPG Books Ltd, Bodmin

CONTENTS

CHAPTER 1

The Primary School

INTRODUCTION

The role of the primary school

Primary schools are everywhere! They provide education for children aged 4–11 across Britain, as the first stage of compulsory schooling. Primary schools are essentially local in character, compared to secondary schools and colleges, and as such have significance beyond their role of providing education for young children.

There are two phases within primary education:

- Infants aged 5–7 years old, in classes Year 1 (Y1) and Year 2 (Y2) learning at Key Stage 1 (KS1) of the National Curriculum.

- Juniors aged 7–11 years old, in classes Year 3, 4, 5 and 6 (Y3, Y4, Y5, Y6) learning at Key Stage 2 (KS2) of the National Curriculum.

The degree of physical separation between the infants and the juniors depends on the individual school. Some schools have infants and juniors integrated in the same building and using the same resources. Others have infants and juniors on the same site, but operating separately. In other situations, the two phases of primary education are in separate schools. In this book, we are focusing directly on the support for teaching and learning at KS1.

Some primary schools also offer nursery grant funded half-day nursery school places to 3- and 4-year-olds, within nursery schools attached to or part of the primary or infant school. These places are free to parents, and they offer nursery education within the Foundation Stage for 3 to 5-year-olds.

Although, legally, children do not have to start school until the term after they reach their fifth birthday, children usually enter school aged 4–5 years, into reception classes. The curriculum for reception classes is within the Foundation Stage, in which children work towards achieving the Early Learning Goals, as do the 3- and 4-year-olds in nursery education. Reception classes are traditionally located within the infants' school, but with the introduction of the Early Learning Goals and the Foundation Stage, some have been relocated to the nursery area of the school.

Primary schools usually offer places to children locally and have strong links with local communities. They are governed by a body of governors, which includes parents, Local Education Authority representatives, the head and teacher governors. The governing body meet regularly to make and ratify decisions about the school, including financial plans, target setting, policies and procedures. Parents are also encouraged to be involved by attending parents' evenings, talking to teachers about any problems, and in some cases, helping out in the classroom. Many parents are involved with fund-raising, parent associations and other aspects of school life.

Primary schools usually have a headteacher and deputy headteacher, unless they are very small. Teachers are class, rather than subject teachers, meaning that a single teacher teaches all subjects to the children in their class, rather than the same subject to children in different classes. Teachers are usually graduates in a Bachelor of Education (B.Ed.) or they are graduates in a curriculum subject, who have completed a Post-graduate Certificate in Education.

Other paid workers in the classroom vary in title, qualifications and job role. They include childcare assistants, teaching assistants and support workers. Their main role is to support children in groups or as individuals either within the class or one to one, and to provide pastoral care particularly for younger children. Some support workers are designated to work with individual children with special educational needs (SEN). Although some classroom assistants are not qualified, others have BTEC or CACHE qualifications or NVQs. It is also possible for some teaching assistants to train to become qualified teachers whilst working within schools.

A *chance to think*

It is important to recognize that primary schools do not exist in a vacuum. The school you work in will be unique in many ways, influenced by the environment in which it exists. It may be an old building, used as a school since the nineteenth century. It may be much newer, purpose-built, and possibly more convenient. It may be rural or urban, in a well-off or less well-off neighbourhood. It may be large or small. Every school will have its own place in the community, based on links with local families and businesses, other education and childcare providers and interested individuals. The type of school, its location and history, the social and economic profile of the neighbourhood, and the people who work in it are all going to have a significant influence on the teaching and learning that takes place.

Exercise 1.1

Do a short profile of your school, with reference to the factors described above. How do you think they influence the teaching and learning that take place? Does the school have any significant problems? What are the school's strong points? Discuss your ideas with a colleague or mentor, and ask them for their perceptions of the school.

1. | THE PRIMARY SCHOOL CURRICULUM

The Education Reform Act, 1988, brought the National Curriculum into being across the maintained school sector, replacing the previous system in which heads or individual teachers could determine what was taught in schools and how it was taught. The National Curriculum covers all stages of compulsory schooling from

5 to 16 years of age. Key Stages 2 and 3 are delivered in secondary schools.

The implementation of the National Curriculum standardized the curriculum in schools to an unprecedented level. For the first time, children in primary schools were learning the same curriculum across England and Wales. The aims of introducing the National Curriculum included improving standards and ensuring children's learning was focused on key skills such as literacy and numeracy.

Initial concerns about the National Curriculum included the heavy emphasis on core subjects (see p. 5) at the expense of foundation subjects (see p. 5) and the prescriptive nature of the teaching and learning. In 1998, guidance was published by the DfEE on the weighting to be given to core and foundation subjects in the light of the introduction of the *Literacy* and *Numeracy Strategies*. The National Curriculum was revised in 1999.

Further developments in the curriculum took place between 1998 and 1999, with the introduction of the National Literacy Strategy and the National Numeracy Strategy. Detailed guidelines on teaching and learning methods and content were published in the *National Literacy Strategy – Framework for Teaching* (DfEE, 1998) and the *National Numeracy Strategy – Framework for Teaching* (DfEE, 1999a). The literacy and numeracy hours were also introduced from 1998 and 1999 respectively, in response to concerns about standards of attainment in these key skills within the British education system. The literacy and numeracy hours are designed to implement the objectives of the strategies, through a practical framework for teaching and learning. The literacy hour at Key Stage 1 is structured as follows:

- 15 minutes whole class shared text work (reading and writing).

- 15 minutes whole class word work.

- 20 minutes group and independent work (independent reading, writing or word work).

- 10 minutes reviewing, reflecting, consolidating teaching and presenting work.

Concerns about the introduction of the literacy hour included reservations about the prescriptive nature of the guidelines and teaching and learning methods, particularly the whole class teaching. However, the guidelines emphasize the need to ensure that whole class teaching is interactive, involving discussion, questioning and responsiveness from the pupils. For example, training and support for teachers delivering the literacy hour includes guidelines on *Talking in Class* (NLS Flier 1, DfEE, 1999b), which offers the teacher a range of strategies for promoting lively and effective classroom discussions.

1.1 The Foundation Stage and the Early Learning Goals

Children aged 3–5 in nursery education and reception classes have their own curriculum and learning goals, designed to support their learning and development, and to provide a basis for successful learning at Key Stage 1 of the National Curriculum. The curriculum for 3- to 5-year-olds was developed to meet the needs of young children in this group in terms of continuity from learning in the home to the requirements of the National Curriculum at Key Stage 1 and above. However, it is important to remember that the Foundation Stage is not just a precursor to the 'real' business of school, but a valid and important stage of learning in itself.

Nursery education is offered in a range of childcare and education settings, which receive nursery grant funding. Traditionally, nursery schools offered pre-school education, but some day nurseries, pre-schools and childminders are now offering nursery education, working towards the Early Learning Goals in the Foundation Stage. The nursery grant funding ensures that free half-day places are offered to 3- and 4-year-olds within these 'educare' settings. The National Child-care Strategy introduced in 1998 has promoted the growth of nursery education places for 3- and 4-year-olds, as part of a wider strategy to increase both the quantity and quality of childcare in the UK.

The *Curriculum Guidance for the Foundation Stage* (QCA, 2000) incorporates learning targets for 3- to 5-year-olds in nursery education and reception classes (the Early Learning Goals), and provides a comprehensive curriculum for three to five-year-olds. The Early Learning Goals (ELGs) are the targets which most children should have achieved by the end of the Foundation Stage, as they enter compulsory education at the age of five. The ELGs are:

- Personal, social and emotional development.

- Communication, language and literacy.

- Mathematical development.

- Knowledge and understanding of the world.

- Physical development.

- Creative development.

Children are expected to reach the ELGs through a series of graded 'stepping stones' — levels of knowledge, skills, understanding and attitudes, which eventually contribute to achieving the ELGs. However, there is a clear recognition that children learn at different rates and have different starting points for their learning within the Foundation Stage.

Key themes within the Foundation Stage are an emphasis on learning through play, informal teaching methods and experiential learning. There is also emphasis on good practice issues, including promoting partnership with parents and other professionals, and meeting the diverse needs of different children, including those with special needs and English as a second language. Learning is integrated in the Foundation Stage, rather than subject based, because research tells us that this approach is better suited to the learning needs of young children.

The transition from the Foundation Stage to Key Stage 1 starts in reception classes, where most children are completing the final steps towards the ELGs, but also starting to develop skills and strategies to tackle the National Curriculum at Key Stage 1. Some children may still be working towards earlier stages of the ELGs by the time they get to reception class.

Children in reception classes follow the *National Literacy and Numeracy Strategies* (QCA, 1998, 1999). The guidelines for the strategies include reception classes, although children within these are not yet on the National Curriculum. The guidelines suggest that literacy and numeracy are not taught in actual 'hours' until later on in the reception year, but that they are taught throughout the day in smaller sessions, in response to the needs of younger children in schools. The introduction of actual 'hours' for literacy and numeracy takes place at some point during the reception year, so that reception class children can become used to the teaching and learning styles they will experience throughout primary school.

There are a number of challenges for reception class management in terms of meeting the requirements of both the Foundation Stage curriculum and preparing children for the National Curriculum at Key Stage 1. This challenge is also rooted in the different teaching and learning styles associated with the Foundation Stage and the National Curriculum. Clearly, reception class teachers need to plan carefully to meet the needs of the children, the requirements of both curricula, and the expectations of both Key Stage 1 and Foundation Stage colleagues. It is, therefore, important for reception class staff to have close links with both the nurseries, to plan for the Foundation Stage, and to the infant classes, to prepare children for Key Stage 1.

1.2 The National Curriculum at Key Stage 1

The National Curriculum became a statutory responsibility for all schools through the Education Reform Act, 1988 (ERA). There are four stages in the National Curriculum. The first stage, Key Stage 1 (KS1) covers the curriculum for pupils aged 5–7 years old.

Core subjects in the National Curriculum are:

- English

- Maths

- Science

Foundation subjects are:

- Art

- Geography

- History

- Music

- PE

- Technology (design technology and information technology).

Each subject has a Programme of Study (PoS) to help teachers plan their delivery and a set of Attainment Targets (ATs) against which teachers can assess progress in individuals' learning and achievements. Information and communications technology (ICT) was a later addition to the National Curriculum supporting the other subjects in the curriculum.

The National Curriculum was developed to provide consistency across England and Wales by providing a standard curriculum for schools, but was also intended to ensure that key subjects such as literacy and numeracy were given full weight within the curriculum. The introduction of literacy and numeracy hours for primary school children and the *Literacy* and *Numeracy Strategies* have supported this approach. Criticisms of the National Curriculum have included the argument that other important subjects are 'squeezed out' by the emphasis on the core subjects. Other criticisms are that the National Curriculum is too prescriptive, not allowing schools to provide for the individual and group needs of their particular pupils.

1.3   Assessment within the National Curriculum

Assessment at the end of each Key Stage is through Standard Assessment Tests (SATs), which are standard national tests for children covering core subjects, and teacher assessment against the Attainment Targets for each subject tested. The teacher judges the child's performance against prescribed standards, which are eight level descriptors of increasing difficulty. Concerns have been expressed about the appropriateness of testing children in this way, particularly the validity of testing 7-year-olds, and whether this constitutes an effective approach to the assessment of young children. Children in Key Stage 1 normally take their KS1 SATs in the May of their Year 2 school year, receiving the results at the end of their school year as part of their final report. Overall results for each school are published in the press as 'league tables', which are used to judge the overall achievement and effectiveness of schools in comparison to each other. However, many factors will affect the outcomes of SATs and the 'league table' effectively results are treated with some caution as a measure of a school's ability to effectively support children's learning.

Schools now have to set and meet targets for SATS results, raising the question as to whether this further reduces the amount of time for teaching and learning the foundation subjects, as testing focuses on the core subjects. Criticisms of target setting include fears that children will be inappropriately 'coached' for the tests at the expense of their broader learning experiences. The Qualifications and Curriculum Authority has produced additional support materials for the teaching of the foundation subjects in order to address these concerns (QCA, 1998).

A *chance to think*

One of the challenges for teaching assistants is to be aware of the experiences children have had before coming into Key Stage 1, and how those experiences may have shaped the child's expectations and responses. Children make transitions from home to pre-school and then to school, and there may be significant changes at each stage, which can affect the child's confidence and ability to learn effectively. While many children will take such changes in their stride, others will be confused and even fearful as new and unexpected demands are made of them.

Exercise 1.2

Consider what you know about the principles and approach of the National Curriculum and also the curriculum for the Foundation Stage. Write down any similarities you are aware of and also any differences. Discuss your ideas with a mentor or colleague and check them against the *National Curriculum for England*, 1999, and the *Curriculum Guidance for the Foundation Stage*, 2000, documents.

2. | THE ROLE OF THE TEACHING ASSISTANT

Introduction

Classrooms are no longer the sole preserve of teachers. In fact, in many classrooms today there is a team of workers delivering the curriculum and assessing children's progress. In one Year 2 literacy hour, which the author recently observed, the team consisted of the teacher, a parent helper working with a small group, a teaching assistant working with an individual child and a specialist teacher working with a group of children who had English as a second language. Primary schools employ a range of support workers who have direct involvement with children's teaching and learning. Confusingly, they may have many different titles, depending on the Local Authority which employs them. These can include education care officers, childcare assistants, support workers, classroom assistants. Some have childcare qualifications such as NNEB, CACHE Diploma, BTEC in Early Childhood Studies, or NVQs. Others are not qualified, but have experience of supporting children's learning. Sometimes support workers work one to one with children with special educational needs (SEN) who require constant care and educational support. Teaching assistants, or classroom assistants, work across a range of classes with groups or individual children, according to the particular needs of children in the school. Their main role may be to support the teacher in delivering Key Stage 1 core subjects.

In addition to supporting children's educational progress, childcare assistants usually have a pastoral care role, which involves helping children with self-care and hygiene, dealing with conflicts and accidents, and applying First Aid. Teaching assistants or childcare assistants may also have organizational responsibilities; including ordering and monitoring supplies of materials, maintaining resources and equipment in good order and ensuring classrooms are tidy, well organized and appropriately equipped. Some teaching assistants are involved in planning teaching and learning activities with the teacher. In other cases, the teacher does the planning, and then discusses methods of delivery and how to achieve differentiation with the support worker. Teaching assistants have an important role in feeding back to teachers in terms of the success or otherwise of a particular activity or lesson.

The role of the teaching assistant has changed over time, bringing increased levels of responsibility and a wider range of tasks. The teaching assistant now has a stronger role in the educational process, as well as the more traditional roles of childcare, preparation, classroom organization and pastoral care. Not only is the role more complex, but it can also vary enormously both within and between schools. Teaching assistants need to be increasingly flexible and innovative in order to meet the varied requirements of their job.

A chance to think

In many schools, the role of the teaching assistant has developed to meet the needs of a more complex and demanding curriculum, larger class sizes and increased levels of formal assessment.

> ## Exercise 1.3
>
> From your own experience and knowledge, jot down a list of the roles and responsibilities a teaching assistant may have in any primary school today. You may be surprised at the extent of the range!

2.1 Qualifications and training

Traditionally, childcare assistants working in primary schools were trained nursery nurses, usually with an NNEB or BTEC childcare qualification. In response to the changing and ever more demanding role of the teaching assistant, new types of training and qualifications have appeared in recent years, aimed at supporting the individual in his or her job by providing opportunities to develop skills, gain new knowledge and become increasingly professional in their approach. Some qualifications have focused on specific aspects of the role. For example, the Specialist Teaching Assistant course offered by CACHE (the Council for Awards in Children's Care and Education) focuses on the role of teaching assistants in delivering and assessing Key Stage 1 English, Maths and Science. Other qualifications are more general, seeking to provide access to basic skills and knowledge, such as NVQs in Early Years Education and Care. The NVQs for Teaching/Classroom Assistants at Level 2 and 3 offer teaching assistants vocational qualifications specifically tailored to their job role (*www.lgnto.org.uk*). However, as yet, many teaching assistants remain unqualified although the majority usually receive some form of training on the job.

Government proposals for extending the role of the teaching assistant will eventually involve new forms of training and qualifications, possibly new routes into teaching for experienced classroom staff. At present, teaching assistants who are graduates can register to become a teacher and train 'on the job', with the agreement and support of the school. However, the new proposals may result in less clear distinctions between teachers and teaching assistants and a more professional role for the latter.

Training opportunities vary between job roles and Local Authorities. Some staff are supported to attend the CACHE Specialist Teaching Assistant courses, while others may be more involved in in-house training. It is important for your professional development to take part in training that is on offer, and to make requests for staff development as required. If it is not clear whether there are such opportunities, or how staff development funding is allocated, clarify this with the appropriate person. At the very least you will signal to the school management that you are keen to develop your skills further.

The *Teaching Assistant's File* (DfEE, 2000) outlines a course of induction training for teaching assistants. This lasts for four days or an equivalent amount of time, and focuses on key areas of support for maths and literacy, behaviour management and personal development. The course is intended to promote a reflective approach to personal and professional development, as discussed further in Chapter 8.

INTRODUCTION

The aim of this handbook is to provide a resource for everyone involved, or considering becoming involved, in working with children in primary schools in the role of a teaching assistant. The role of support staff in schools has become increasingly important with the growth of class sizes and the ever-increasing complexity of the primary curriculum. The responsibilities of teaching assistants have grown apace with these changes and now cover a wide range of classroom and school-wide, educational and pastoral activities. Plans to extend the role of teaching assistants to free teachers for other tasks include expectations that teaching assistants will eventually be directly responsible for whole classroom teaching and management (*Observer*, 11 November 2001).

Amongst their many functions, teaching assistants are carers, educators, planners, assessors and counsellors, and in many cases, the 'glue' which holds together the diverse activities of a busy primary school. In the *Guardian Education* (8 May 2001), Laura Barton points out that teaching assistants not only work with groups of children and provide physical care, they also plan lessons, attend reviews of children with special educational needs, and write reports and daily records on these children. In addition, they must become computer literate, and learn to communicate through sign language and with children who have different first languages to their own. They must also be familiar with the demands of the National Curriculum and the literacy and numeracy strategies.

Despite the range and complexity of the role, teaching assistants are poorly paid and often unqualified, although 35 per cent do have professional qualifications and 6 per cent have a degree (*Guardian Education*, 20 November 2001). A survey by the Professional Association of Nursery Nurses found classroom assistants 'endured low pay and status' and 'despite their expertise and wide-ranging responsibilities, and even with appropriate training and qualifications, the classroom assistants surveyed earned only £9,531 to £12,444 and most were required to work extra hours without extra pay' (*Guardian Education Letters*, 15 May 2001). Despite these limitations, many find the role of teaching assistant rewarding and worthwhile.

Non-teacher staff in classrooms have many different titles – teaching assistants, childcare assistants, classroom assistants, education care officers, support workers, teacher's aides, link workers and specialist teaching assistants are some examples. A few of these titles relate to childcare qualified workers with qualifications such as BTECs, NNEBs or CACHE Diplomas, but in practice the range of tasks is much the same for qualified and unqualified workers, whatever their title. For example, one of the author's students, a teaching assistant with a BTEC in Early Childhood Studies qualification, planned and delivered differentiated work to small groups within the literacy and numeracy hours, worked one-to-one with children with special needs, provided physical care and pastoral care, general classroom support in nursery, infants and juniors across a range of schools – all under the grand title of 'locum nursery nurse'!

The term teaching assistant has been applied to staff who support teachers delivering the core curriculum subjects. However, recently, the term teaching assistant has been used more widely referring to all classroom support staff – in discussions about the expanding role of non-teacher qualified staff in classrooms.

For the purposes of this handbook, the term teaching assistant will be used most commonly, in reference to both qualified and unqualified workers.

Many parents also become volunteer classroom helpers, supporting individual children and groups with reading and other tasks, helping with creative activities such as cooking, art, sewing and assisting on trips out and other events. Current thinking, based on research, supports the view that parental involvement and partnerships between parents and schools helps children to succeed in their learning and can support the work of the school. These ideas are a common thread running through discussions on how the curriculum in nurseries and primary schools should be delivered. Some teaching assistants start out as parent volunteers; others are trained nursery nurses who have been childcare assistants in schools for some years, still others are staff who have been working with children in a range of capacities.

This handbook is designed as a basic text for anyone working with children in schools in a teaching assistant capacity, or for anyone who is considering doing this role. It is aimed at both new and experienced staff in primary schools. The main emphasis will be on the role of teaching assistants supporting teachers working with children aged 5–7-years-old at Key Stage 1 (KS1) of the National Curriculum. These are pupils in either infant schools or the infant classes of primary schools. KS1 of the National Curriculum is taught in Year 1 (Y1) and Year 2 (Y2) classes. Reception classes for 4–5 year olds follow the curriculum for 3–5-year-olds in the Foundation Stage. This curriculum is aimed at helping children achieve the Early Learning Goals, which are the learning targets for children aged 3–5 years old (QCA, 2000). Although the focus of this book is mainly on working with children at KS1, the Early Learning Goals in the Foundation Stage will be referred to in terms of their link with KS1 and the role of the Foundation Stage in preparing children for KS1, as well as providing young children with a curriculum to meet their specific needs. Many classroom assistants in primary or infant schools work across the range of age groups, and therefore need to have knowledge and understanding of both the National Curriculum (QCA, 1999) and the Foundation Stage (QCA, 2000).

Some key themes run throughout the book. These include basic skills for teaching assistants, such as communication skills, working with others and professionalism. Professionalism simply means the ways in which teaching assistants learn to work within the requirements of their employer and the job role they are employed to fulfil. 'Being professional' can include behaving objectively, putting your own feelings and opinions aside, responding to others politely and courteously, following procedures and guidelines, and working within a job description and the expectations of your employers. It can also mean challenging poor standards of practice in the workplace and developing a critical approach to evaluating work practices. In this context, 'a critical approach' means developing the ability to question established work practices and consider whether they are the best approach. Just because we have been doing something in a particular way for a long time does not mean it is the right way! Clearly, to develop a 'critical approach', you need to keep up-to-date with developments in child education and be aware of current issues in the field. So, professionalism is also about self-development and awareness of change.

Another key theme is working with children with special educational needs (SEN). The book does not have a specific chapter on children with SEN, because the discussion about the needs of these children and how they can be met is integrated into each chapter. However, there is a section in Chapter 1 where the role of teaching assistants with children with SEN is outlined as an introduction. Teaching assistants have a key role working with children with SEN outside the classroom on a one-to-one basis, and also the very important role of helping children with SEN to integrate into the mainstream curriculum.

The contents of this handbook are aimed primarily at supporting staff studying for the CACHE Specialist Teaching Assistant Award (www.cache.org.uk), but are also linked to the requirements of other relevant courses of study, including the NVQ's for Teaching/Classroom Assistants (www.lgnto.org.uk). The handbook also provides basic information for teaching assistants who are planning to do a sector-endorsed Foundation Degree. These newer qualifications, based in universities and their partner colleges, are designed for people working with young children in the early years who wish to take a degree level course while remaining in work. Sector-endorsed Foundation Degrees can confer 'senior practitioner' status on students who successfully achieve a range of competencies built into the course. Completion of a Foundation Degree provides the opportunity to progress to the final stage of an Honours degree, for example, in Early Childhood Studies, and possibly initial teacher training. However, the handbook also provides anyone working within a primary classroom with important information about their roles and responsibilities, and how to extend their knowledge and understanding of these to the classroom.

Within the text, boxes can be found entitled A Chance to Think, which contain more detailed reflections on a particular issue or aspect, and exercises for the reader to complete. These exercises are designed to offer the reader a chance to consider key issues more deeply and to develop a reflective approach to their work. Although many of the exercises are on work-based themes, they are also suitable for readers who are not yet in employment within a school. However, any inexperienced individual who is planning to become a teaching assistant is advised to consider volunteering in a school.

Some of the exercises have sample answers for you to compare to your own answers. These can be found in the appendices at the end of the book. It is important to remember, however, that for many of the exercises there are no 'right' or 'wrong' answers. The aim of the exercises is to promote thinking and reflection, and to develop analytical skills (a 'critical approach') as discussed in Chapter 8. For some readers, the exercises will provide a useful framework for the development of the self-reflective accounts, which are course requirements for some qualifications.

In order to make the handbook more accessible, the chapters cover specific areas. The handbook is designed as a source to be 'dipped into' and re-read, as well as a basic text. Each chapter offers a range of references and suggested reading to support the reader in extending his or her knowledge through additional study.

In order to help you relate the contents of each chapter to your own work practices, case studies and examples drawn from observations are included to illustrate some areas of the text. These are drawn from 'real-life' events, which took place in a range of schools, including detailed experiences of teaching assistants. It is useful to compare your own experiences to those of others, but obviously the children's identity has been protected.

The book also contains a Glossary. Although jargon is kept to the minimum, inevitably there are words and phrases, acronyms and shorthand terminology which are frequently used in schools and by education professionals, and which the reader needs to be aware of. In parts of the text where an acronym is to be used more than once, the full name will be given on the first occasion, followed by the acronym in brackets and on subsequent occasions of use, the acronym alone will be used, e.g., Local Education Authority (LEA). However, all such terms will be in the Glossary, so if in doubt, look it up!

Finally, to avoid the cumbersome device of using dual gender terms, such as 'he and/or she' or 's/he', male or female gender has been randomly assigned to children and adults referred to in the text, on a roughly equal basis.

The chapters work together to give an overview of the teaching assistant's role in supporting children, mainly at KS1, but they can also be read separately to provide information about specific issues. The Contents and 'Index' can be used to access different topics within the book.

NOTES FOR FURTHER READING

Barton, L. (2001)
'Many Hands' *Guardian Education*, 8 May, *Guardian Unlimited*.
www.guardian.co.uk/schools/story/0,5500,487161,00.html

Council for Awards in Children's Care and Education (CACHE) (1999)
'Specialist Teaching Assistant Award', September 2000.
www.cache.org.uk

Hinscliff, G. (2001)
'Untrained staff get key teaching role'.
Observer, 11 November 2001, *Guardian Unlimited*.
www.guardian.co.uk/Archive/Article/0,4273,4296638,00.html

Local Government Training Organisation (2001)
'National Vocational Qualifications for Teaching/Classroom Assistants'.
www.lgnto.org.uk

Pritchard, T. (2001)
'Chartered Assistants?' *Guardian Education Letters*, 15 May,
Guardian Unlimited.
www.guardian.co.uk/Archive/Article/0,4273,4186231,00.html

Qualifications and Curriculum Authority (1999)
'National Curriculum for England' QCA/DfEE.
www.nc.uk.net

Qualifications and Curriculum Authority (2000)
'Curriculum guidance for the Foundation Stage'.
www.nc.uk.net

Saddington, S. (2001)
'Taking Offence' *Guardian Education*, 20 November, *Guardian Unlimited*.
www.guardian.co.uk/Archive/Article/0,4273,4302384,00.html

2.2 Supporting children with special educational needs

Children with special educational needs are identified and supported according to a set of requirements outlined in the Code of Practice for Special Educational Needs. It is a legal requirement for Local Education Authorities (LEAs) and schools to assess and meet the needs of children identified as having SEN, according to the guidelines within the Code of Practice. Once children are identified as having SEN at Level 3 or above, the teacher and the Special Education Needs Co-ordinator (SENCO), in partnership with parents and other relevant professionals, draw up an Individual Education Plan (IEP) for them. The IEP is reviewed at regular intervals and new targets for achievement are set and monitored. The school should have a special educational needs policy that outlines how children with SEN will be supported in school, in line with the Code of Practice and relevant legislation. It is important that you familiarize yourself with these documents and ask any questions you have about them. Many such policies emphasize partnership with parents and an inclusive approach to meeting the needs of children with SEN. There is also a school governor who is responsible for school-wide SEN issues through the board of governors.

Teaching assistants are frequently involved in working on a one-to-one or small group basis with children with SEN, in line with the child or children's individual targets. Supporting small groups of children with SEN in the classroom is a major role for most teaching assistants. Some children with more severe SEN or physical disabilities may have long-term daily support from a specific support worker who works with the child in the class and on a one-to-one basis.

Although teaching assistants have many skills in working with children with SEN, they are not always provided with all the relevant information about the child, therefore you may need to ask or to let the SENCO or teacher know that you do not feel adequately informed. Roffey has drawn up a useful checklist of questions that could be asked to clarify the involvement of support staff with children with SEN:

How often will the support assistant be in the classroom?

How will exact days and times be negotiated?

What is the support assistant there to do?

How does this fit in with the child's IEP?

Who decides the day-to-day role of the support assistant?

What should be the balance between individual work and group work?

How will the child's inclusion into the class be supported by the assistant?

Will the support assistant be spending time out of the classroom? How often, and what is the explicit purpose of this?

What liaison time needs to be made available for the class teacher and the support assistant to meet together? When will this be?

How often should regular meetings with parents, the SENCO, the class teacher and the support assistant take place? Who will arrange this?

(Roffey, 1999: 101)

> ## A chance to think
>
> Knowing the extent and limits of your own roles and responsibilities is an important part of gaining confidence and expertise in working with children with SEN.
>
> ## Exercise 1.4
>
> Using the checklist above, try and answer the questions about your role with one or more of the children with SEN you are involved in supporting. If you are not able to answer all the questions, ask the SENCO or the teacher.

There is an important emphasis on teamwork and a multi-agency approach to supporting children with SEN, and the teaching assistant's role will always be in the context of this. Other significant professionals working with children with SEN can include:

- Educational psychologists – employed by the LEA to assess children's special educational needs and suggest strategies to support the child in school.

- Speech therapists – employed by the local Health Authority to support children's language development.

- Physiotherapists and occupational therapists – normally employed by the Health Authority to support children's physical development, co-ordination, balance and mobility.

- Social workers – employed by the Local Authority Social Services Department to support children in need and children at risk of abuse, and their families. Children with disabilities, either physical or learning, are usually assessed as 'children in need'. Under the Children Act, 1989, the Local Authority, through its social services provision, has a duty to identify such children's needs and to meet them as far as is possible, in co-operation with other agencies such as education.

- LEA peripatetic services for children with visual and hearing impairment – qualified specialist teachers employed to support children, parents and teachers in schools and at home.

There may be many other types of professionals involved with specific children you work with. It is important to identify their role with the child and the responsibilities they may have within their agency. It can, however, be difficult sometimes when you attend an IEP review meeting, to determine who is who, especially if you have just started working with the child. Many of us have sat through meetings not daring to speak because we are not sure of who we are speaking to! It is good practice for the SENCO, or whoever else chairs the meeting, to ensure that introductions are made at the beginning of the meeting. If she or he forgets, gently remind her or him that you are not sure who everyone is. Other staff or the parents may be equally baffled and grateful that you have spoken up. Working with parents of children with SEN requires particular skills in dealing with the feelings and difficulties to which their parents are subject. For many parents, having a child with SEN has become a long battle for resources and appropriate support by the time the child reaches school age. For others, the realization that their child has SEN may have come at a later stage, and they may still be coming to terms with the fact that their child needs extra help.

Roffey (1999: 7) suggests that 'Finding the right balance between acknowledgement of the parents' emotional response, the reality of the situation and being positive about the possibilities is not easy.'

Special educational needs have multiple causes and, in a sense, it is inappropriate to lump all children with SEN together as a single group. The brief examples listed below illustrate the wide variety of children who are deemed to have SEN:

- Brendon, 5, is deaf in one ear and has partial hearing in the other.

- David, 6, is partially blind.

- Gavin, 7, has learning and physical developmental delays associated with extreme neglect in his first two years of life.

- Shelley, 5, has no speech, movement problems and major learning difficulties.

- Susan, 6, is currently on the Child Protection Register for physical abuse and neglect. She has global learning difficulties and delays in her social and emotional development.

Supporting children with special educational needs requires a good knowledge of the child's needs and how they are to be met, as outlined in the IEP. It is also useful to have knowledge of the range of support the child is receiving from other agencies and professionals and how this fits in with your role.

Good relationships with parents are key elements in supporting the child and ensuring that he or she receives the best quality help. Parents often benefit from a good relationship with teaching assistants who work with their child. The knowledge that their child is being supported by a committed, professional and knowledgeable individual can be a great help in reducing anxiety and helping parents feel more positive.

2.3 Other roles for teaching assistants

Teaching assistants may be employed in other roles within a school. In multi-lingual schools, teaching assistants may be employed because they are bi- or multi-lingual and they then may have a specific role in supporting children who do not have English as a first language. Other specialist skills may include signing in Makaton or British Sign Language, supporting children with specific care needs, disabilities or illnesses.

Some support staff in schools often have other, more general duties. These can involve some of the following:

- Keeping classrooms tidy, attractive and safe.

- Making and arranging displays of work.

- Supporting teachers on trips out.

- Arranging or supporting school art and drama events.

- Arranging or supporting out-of-school events such as discos, school fairs and sports events.

- Ordering supplies and ensuring materials are available as required.

And many, many other tasks! The role of support staff in schools can vary enormously, both between staff and within one staff member's job role. For example, a childcare assistant in one school, who has a nursery nurse qualification and who also successfully achieved the CACHE Specialist Teaching Assistant Award, supports groups of children in and out of class as a teaching assistant; works with individual children; provides support and help for sick and injured children; arranges displays throughout the school; organizes school trips and helps on them; arranges out-of-school events such as the disco; contributes to the school fair; attends governors' meetings as the support staff governor and a myriad of other tasks.

Perhaps the most important point is that each of you knows what is expected of you in your own specific job role, and that you develop the skills and abilities to perform your role well and to develop within the job role.

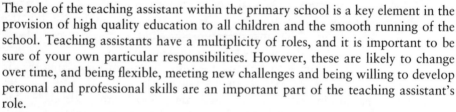

CONCLUSIONS

The role of the teaching assistant within the primary school is a key element in the provision of high quality education to all children and the smooth running of the school. Teaching assistants have a multiplicity of roles, and it is important to be sure of your own particular responsibilities. However, these are likely to change over time, and being flexible, meeting new challenges and being willing to develop personal and professional skills are an important part of the teaching assistant's role.

Knowing about the school, the community and other significant agencies and professionals is important in terms of being able to view your own role in the context of others. Taking up staff development opportunities, being aware of school policies and major government policy or guidance documents is also a significant step towards developing a professional approach to your work. In the light of proposed developments in the teaching assistant's role, working towards a professional, reflective approach is more important than ever.

Notes for further reading

DfEE (1998)
National Literacy Strategy – Framework for Teaching. Nottingham: DfEE Publications Centre.

DfEE (1999a)
National Numeracy Strategy – Framework for Teaching. Nottingham: DfEE Publications Centre.

DfEE (1999b)
'Talking in Class' National Literacy Strategy 1. Nottingham: DfEE Publications Centre.

DfEE (2000)
Teaching Assistant's File.
Nottingham: DfEE Publications Centre.

Qualifications and Curriculum Authority (QCA) (1998)
Maintaining Breadth and Balance at Key Stage 1 and 2.
Sudbury: QCA.

Qualifications and Curriculum Authority (QCA) (1999)
Investing in our Future: Early Learning Goals.
Sudbury: QCA.

Qualifications and Curriculum Authority (QCA) (1999)
National Curriculum for England.
Sudbury: QCA.
QCA/DfEE also at *www.National Curriculum. uk.net*

Qualifications and Curriculum Authority (QCA) (2000)
Curriculum Guidance for the Foundation Stage.
Sudbury: QCA.

Roffey, S. (1999)
Special Needs in the Early Years
London. David Fulton.

CHAPTER 2

How Children Learn

INTRODUCTION

One of the most important keys to understanding the best ways of supporting young children's learning development is to recognize the ways in which young children learn best. Every decision about what and how children are taught contains a view of how children learn. This view may not always be clearly stated, but it is implicit in the process of planning teaching and learning. For example, a teacher could choose to discuss a science experiment with the class, write about the experiment on the board and then demonstrate the experiment to the class. Or she could ask the children how they could find out something about the natural or physical world, discuss their ideas on how to do the experiment, help them to set up and complete the experiment and then encourage them to evaluate their findings. Each of these approaches is based on a different view of how children learn best.

This chapter will explore theories about how children learn and the ways these theories have influenced our approach to supporting young children's learning development in schools. It will also examine the role of play in learning and the individual needs of children who learn at different rates within a group. The particular learning needs of children with special educational needs (SEN) and those with disabilities are discussed, as are the needs of children who are multilingual or bilingual. The adult role in responding to differentiated learning needs is another theme, including the teaching assistant's need to have a sound understanding of individual children's learning and overall development.

Learning is only one aspect of young children's development and it is important to acknowledge that children do not develop in compartments, but that different aspects of their development are inextricably linked. For example, when a child is first entering school, the level of his social and emotional development and any impairment or delay in his physical development will influence the stage of learning development he or she is at. In addition, common sense tells us that a child's experience outside, as well as inside, the school environment will also influence his or her holistic development. Bronfenbrenner's ecological model places the child at the heart of a system of influences, which includes family and friends, social and cultural influences, the economic situation, work and employment and health of different family members. All these factors will influence the child's development either directly or through the impact they have on the child's carers (Bronfenbrenner, 1979).

For example, the illness or unemployment of a parent may lead to stress or depression among the adults in the family, perhaps exacerbated by problems with money, strains on relationships and conflict within the family. These factors may have an impact on both the quality and quantity of interactions between the adults and the child. Parents may have less time and energy to play or talk with their child, to read and listen or to show warmth and affection. Discipline may become more inconsistent or authoritarian. This may impact on the child's confidence and self-esteem or on his or her sense of 'belongingness'. As a result, the child may feel less able to tackle new tasks or to risk making mistakes. The child may be less confident in a group and may communicate less frequently. The net result may be that the child's ability to use learning opportunities is reduced and learning development is slowed.

It is important to recognize that many complex factors may influence the rate and range of a child's development and that children do not develop evenly or at the same rate as each other.

1. THEORIES OF LEARNING

Perhaps one of the best-known theorists in this field is Jean Piaget. Piaget's work laid a solid foundation for subsequent theories which influence approaches to teaching and learning as it is today. Piaget theorized that children need to actively explore their environment to begin to understand it. Children from babyhood onwards interact with their environment using their senses and growing physical skills to learn about their world. Think of a baby who is starting to crawl. She/he will move towards objects that attract her/his attention through sound, motion, colour or smell. She/he will try and grasp or touch the object, put it in her/his mouth or move it about. For example, she may pick up a rattle, shake it, chew it, throw it or bang it on the floor. In this way, she/he is learning about what the rattle does and what can be done with it, through her/his own investigation. So, Piaget believed that children were not passive in their learning. He supported the view that children learned through their own experiences and actions, which provided them with the knowledge to constantly revise and adjust their understanding of the world around them. However, it is important to remember that 'active learning' is not just about physical movement and action, but also about active thinking and reflection on new experiences to try and make sense of them. It is this part of the learning process which adults can focus on, helping children to think about and make sense of their experiences (Hurst and Joseph, 1998: 20).

Piaget theorized that children progress through a series of stages in their learning, which are linked but not tied to different age groups. According to Piaget, children cannot leap from stage to stage, but gradually move from one stage to the next in an invariable sequence. Piaget saw the child as having mental models, which he described as 'schema', which incorporate the child's understanding of the world. New experiences give the child a chance to 'assimilate' new knowledge. However, new information creates what Piaget referred to as 'disequilibrium', which is an imbalance between what the child already understands (her existing 'schema') and the knowledge he/she has gained through new experiences. The process of 'accommodating' new information by altering existing schema to include the new knowledge means that the child reaches equilibrium again. Through this constantly repeated process, the child gains an increasingly complex and sophisticated understanding of his/her environment.

Piaget defined several stages of cognitive development in young children, linked to different ages. They are:

- **Sensorimotor stage** (0–2 years) – children explores the world through their physical movements and their senses. For example, a baby gripping a plastic rattle, shaking and chewing it.

- **Pre-operational stage** (2–7 years) – children are learning about the world around them and are making connections, but do not yet think logically.

- **Concrete operational stage** (7–11) – children can apply logical thinking to the actual experiences or situations they are involved in.

- **Formal operational stage** (11–adulthood) – children can think logically about abstract issues or problems.

Piaget's ideas have been criticized, despite their influence on how children are taught in schools. Criticisms tend to relate to Piaget's emphasis on what children cannot do, rather than what they can do. Piaget's view that children cannot learn at the next stage until they are ready was also challenged by other theorists who believed that children can be supported and encouraged to develop to a higher level of ability sooner than if left until 'ready'.

The pre-operational stage is often cited in terms of this criticism. Piaget argued that at this stage, children are unable to think logically and that they are 'egocentric' – unable to see the world from another's point of view. However, critics argue that Piaget's experiments, on which his theories are based, were flawed and did not conclusively point to the conclusions he drew. Further experiments showed that when children are faced with a context they understand, they are able to see the world from another's point of view.

Margaret Donaldson (1978) was influential in encouraging educationalists to recognize that children learn best in a 'meaningful context'. Children need to understand the reasons why they are involved in particular activities, and to be able to relate those activities to their existing understanding. Although children do not continue to learn through practical activities throughout their school life, they need to be helped to move gradually towards 'abstract learning'. Donaldson's ideas are still very important in terms of the approaches used to help young children learn, particularly the emphasis placed on first-hand experiences and learning through play. These principles are embedded in the approach to teaching and learning outlined in the *Curriculum Guidance for the Foundation Stage* for 3- to 5-year-olds (QCA, 2000).

Perhaps the most influential theorist at the beginning of the twenty-first century is Lev Vygotsky (1978), whose ideas have contributed a great deal to our understanding of how children learn. Vygotsky recognized important links between language and communication and cognitive development, and he emphasized the social nature of learning. He believed that the basis of learning lay in the interactions children have with others. He particularly emphasized the importance of support for learning, and argued that children reached higher levels of achievement when supported by adults or more experienced children. Vygotsky developed the notion of the 'zone of proximal development' (ZPD) to explain this theory. The ZPD is the next stage of development, which a child is moving towards. Support helps the child to move into his/her ZPD, through the help and support of more experienced others. Vygotsky also believed that children operate at their highest level of ability during play, demonstrating skills, knowledge and understanding not seen during other examples of the child's activities or behaviour. Vygotsky argued that children were a 'head taller' during play, particularly imaginative play, where all the child's knowledge, skills and abilities come together to demonstrate a higher level of development than may have been previously observed.

For example, Declan, 6, was playing at 'quarantining' the playroom during an outbreak of disease among farm animals. Declan did not write at home, and was very reluctant to involve himself in writing activities in school. After 'fencing' off the room with a variety of materials, Declan asked his mother for a sign to keep people out. She drew a cross on a small piece of paper. Declan asked for a sign with the words 'no entry' on it. His mother wrote 'no entry' on another small piece of paper. Exasperated, he snatched up a large piece of paper and wrote 'no entry' on it, carefully copying the script and producing the first writing he had ever completed voluntarily.

Jerome Bruner argued that children's learning is strongly influenced by their social and cultural environment (Bruner, 1966). The content and type of learning depends very much on the culture the child develops within, and the child's schema will develop in ways that are influenced by that culture. Like Vygotsky, Bruner was strongly in favour of supporting children's learning with help as required. He described this as 'scaffolding', using the image of a scaffold to support the child's learning until it is firmly in place and the scaffolding can be removed, bit by bit (Wood *et al.*, 1976). Bruner also introduces the concept of a spiral curriculum, which portrays how children can start to learn about different aspects of the curriculum at any stage and then revisit these at a later stage and learn about more complex and extensive aspects of the topic or theme. For example, a young child may initially learn scientific principles about the effect of heat on materials through cooking activities. The child may notice and discuss how foods change when heat is applied. At a later stage, he may conduct scientific experiments that involve changing other materials through the application of heat.

2. | CHILDREN AS LEARNERS

There are several processes involved in children's learning, which can be identified and worked with to support the child's progress. Merry (1998: 32) described successful learning as: 'a set of overlapping processes where learners actively seek out new information, select from it, transform it, impose meaning on it and evaluate it in the light of what they already know'. However, it is important to remember that children cannot and do not process all the information which comes their way. They have limited concentration spans and cannot focus on the myriad of new information which they experience all the time. Children cannot remember everything and many things are not stored in their long-term memories. In order to make sense of new information children use past experience and knowledge. This means that they sometimes make incorrect assumptions about new information or jump to the wrong conclusions.

2.1 The influence of theory on how we support children's learning

Theories can be hard to understand in abstract, or it may be that we can grasp the principles of a particular theory and then wonder how it applies to our day-to-day activities. Sometimes we work in particular ways because we know they are 'right' or they work, but we would not easily be able to explain why this is the case. These ways of working, which draw on observation and experience, may have a theoretical basis which is not explicit, but which still informs our approach. Yet theories such as Piaget's, Bruner's and Vygotsky's have had a great deal of influence on the ways in which we support the learning of young children. Some of these influences include:

- Emphasis on first-hand experiences in early learning, and the role of adults in providing opportunities for new experiences.

- Recognition of the importance of questions, conversations and communication about the child's experiences in order to make sense of these and help the child absorb them into his/her understanding.

- Recognition of the value of the social nature of learning, in terms of all aspects of the child's development.

- Acknowledgement of the importance of learning through play as a medium for developing all aspects of the child's knowledge, understanding, language, social and problem-solving skills.

- Incorporating the concept of the spiral curriculum in curriculum planning at all stages, building on a child's earlier experiences and knowledge to develop understanding further.

A chance to think

Understanding the influence of theory on practice helps us to understand 'why we do the things we do', and the basis on which planning should take place. It informs our approach to all aspects of supporting children's learning and helps us understand how we can best achieve good standards in the classroom. Theory can also help us to tackle problems with individual children or groups, where learning is not effectively taking place. It can help us to evaluate the usefulness of different approaches.

Exercise 2.1

Read the short scenarios below and comment on them with reference to the theories discussed above. How effective is the learning experience described? What aspects of the child's development may it support? How could the activity be varied or developed to provide better learning opportunities?

1. A group of 5-year-olds are painting. Davey spends a lot of time layering different colours across his sheet of paper until it is soaked. Then he lifts the paper and starts to twist and turn it, declaring that he intends to model a dinosaur. He comments on how the different colours run together into a spiral as he twists.

2. A group of 4-year-olds are each given a cut-out fish shape. They are provided with glue and brushes, crinkled tissue paper and glitter glue. The children decorate the fish shapes with adult advice and support.

3. Pupils in a Year 2 class have been looking at transport as a topic. In small groups, they are asked to plan and model a vehicle for transporting people or goods. The pupils have access to a wide range of modelling materials, including paper, card, glue, modelling clay.

Compare your answers with the sample answers on page 163.

2.2 Language and learning

The role of language in learning is central. Children learn through their conversations with adults because in this way they are able to make sense of the world around them. The type and quality of the communication is crucial. Children need to have genuine and meaningful discussions and conversations with adults and peers in order to make sense of their world. These conversations start in the home from a very early age as parents talk and listen to their children about everything that they experience or think about. If you are travelling on a bus or sitting in a park, you will hear these everyday conversations going on between parents and their children. You will have had them yourself. These conversations not only help to develop children's language skills through extending vocabulary, but they also offer the child a means to explore ideas and concepts, learn new things, solve problems and think in new ways. They are a crucial aspect of children's learning development. However, Tizard and Hughes (1984) found that the use of language in schools is different to that at home. In school, adults often use conversation to test children's knowledge rather than to discuss and explain ideas and experiences. The quality of the conversation may not be of the same standard as that at home. Listening to the child is very important in understanding what the conversation is about and in judging the sort of response that will extend a child's thinking and understanding. Many of us have probably had experience of misjudging the child's interest, starting a long explanation and then realizing that we have lost our audience in the first sentence!

Bruner argued that children not only learn language from adults, but that they use language to promote all aspects of their development (Bruner, 1983). Vygotsky (1978) believed that language and cognitive development are closely linked. The development of language influences how we think and what we think about. Bruner believed that this was closely linked to how children learn about their own culture. The process of learning to think is promoted by what Vygotsky (1978) called 'inner speech' where children describe to themselves what they are doing, in order to make sense of it and commit it to memory. This 'inner speech' gradually becomes internalized as children's thought processes develop further. In this way, the acquisition of language helps the development of thinking, which is crucial in learning.

2.3   Multilingual and bilingual children

It is important to be aware that children who have English as a second or subsequent language may have difficulty accessing learning in an environment which is dominated by a different culture to their home culture. Learning development is strongly influenced by language development, which is based on culture. The type of learning a child will have been involved in at home will depend on the family's culture and how this is interpreted through the home language. This means that children from British minority cultures may not only have to learn in English as a subsequent language, but also have to learn in a different way to that which they are used to. Practitioners need to be sensitive to the need to ensure all children's previous learning is valued, and that children may have very different learning styles.

3.   SUPPORTING CHILDREN'S LEARNING AND DEVELOPMENT

The adult role

There are many different ideas about the role of adults in supporting children's learning and development. Some, such as Piaget, argue that the adult's main role is to provide a stimulating and safe environment for children to explore and learn in. Others believe the adult's role should be more pro-active. As discussed previously, Vygotsky (1978) argued that learning is a social experience, and that children learn best with the support of peers or adults. Adults can closely observe the child's activity and offer relevant support to help the child function at the next stage of his/her development (the ZPD).

One of the ways in which this can be done is by modelling an activity or skills. Children learn new things from each other all the time in this way. For example, Amy, seven, learned a new clapping song whilst on holiday. When she went back to school she introduced the clapping song to a friend. A group of children in the playground observed and copied the routine, and then practiced with each other until word-perfect. They then taught the routine to literally dozens of other children in the school over the next few weeks, until the clapping song was part of the school repertoire.

Bruner's concept of 'scaffolding' is important in terms of our understanding of the adult role. Like Vygotsky, Bruner believed that children learn best when adults help and support them. Scaffolding refers to the support that adults can offer to children to help them achieve beyond their current ability. Scaffolding often involves breaking tasks down into smaller stages and then helping children at each stage until they can complete the whole task confidently. This could involve modelling, or instructing, planning and discussing methods or working alongside a child (Wood *et al.*, 1976).

For example, a 5-year-old girl, Harriet, wants to make a birthday card for her brother. The adult shows Harriet an old birthday card and demonstrates how the paper is folded to make the card. Harriet folds her paper, but it is skewed. The adult uses the old card to show Harriet how to line up the corners to get a neat fold, explaining how this is done as she demonstrates. The second time round the card is folded neatly. The adult and the child then discuss the card, looking at what is written on the old card and where it is written, the images used and where they are placed. The adult and the child plan together to decide what will go in the new card and where each piece of writing or image will go. They then go on to discuss whether drawing, painting or collage will look best. In this step-by-step way, Harriet gradually learns the process of making a card, supported by the adult. The next time Harriet makes a card, she may still need help, but she will gradually become more confident and independent in this area.

It is important to note the role of conversation in this process. The child is not asked to guess at what the adult is doing and why she is doing it. The adult explains his/her purposes and actions throughout the sequence. Children cannot learn just through observation because the underlying principles or processes might not be obvious. The adult needs to give this explanation in order to ensure the child is clear about the processes. Merry (1998) suggests that the adult emphasizes the most important parts of the process and does not behave like an expert, so the child has a chance to understand each part of the activity or process.

Bruner and Vygotsky both saw interaction between the adult and the child as an important part of the learning process, as long as the intervention is relevant and supportive. Inappropriate intervention can cause confusion or frustration, or simply put the child off completing the activity or task. Adults need to be careful not to impose their own agenda when supporting learning, for example, by over-emphasizing the use of literacy and numeracy skills or telling the child how to complete a task where the real learning is in the child problem-solving for himself.

A chance to think

In order to effectively support children's learning it is important to be sure of whether intervention is appropriate and welcome. Trying to help a child who is coping alone, or leaving intervention until the child has become frustrated or lost interest is not effective. The timing, type and extent of intervention to support children with learning activities depend on accurate judgements about what is needed. In order to make these judgements, the adult needs a lot of information about what the child is doing and what he is interested in achieving. If the adult intervenes without this information, they may simply get it wrong and not help the child at all.

For example, Becky, 6, was recording in her 'diary' after the weekend. The classroom assistant, knowing that Becky was not a confident writer, sat with her and asked Becky what she was recording. Becky said she was drawing a picture of the family's camper van, in which they had gone away for the weekend. The classroom assistant suggested that she wrote some words about the weekend which Becky could copy. Becky didn't reply – she was half way through her drawing and the help she was being offered was not what she needed at that point in time.

Observation and assessment skills are crucial to ensure that support for children's learning is both timely and appropriate.

> ### Exercise 2.2
>
> Choose an example from your experience of supporting children in the classroom. Make notes, recording the type of help offered and how effective it was.
>
> 1. What factors influenced the effectiveness of the support given?
>
> 2. What could have been done differently to further support the child or children?
>
> Ensure that your suggestions are relevant and appropriate to the child's needs.
>
> Discuss your findings with a colleague or mentor.

3.1 The role of play in learning and development

In the eighteenth and nineteenth centuries, play was largely seen as an alternative to work or as a mechanism for children to 'blow off steam' and release excess energy. Educational pioneers such as Froebel, Isaacs and MacMillan, recognized that for young children play is an essential medium for exploration and learning and for the development of all aspects of the child's physical and cognitive abilities. Their work was important in changing the way children were cared for and educated in the nineteenth and early twentieth century.

Play is traditionally considered to provide children with a significant context for development in which they can explore and learn, gain social and language skills through group play and learn to express and control emotions. However, there is little 'hard evidence' in the shape of research findings to support this view, and the theories, which underpin the value of play in learning, are many and contradictory. Consequently, the role of play in education is often seen as under attack from the increased formalization of the curriculum for young children and the demands of the National Curriculum, SATs and the literacy and numeracy hours (Bruce, 1991). In schools, teachers express support for the notion of learning through play, but in practice play is often an afterthought or something to do when the work is done (Bennett *et al.*, 1997).

Some research does support the view that sociodramatic play (role play with more than one child) involves complex communication about rules, including negotiation skills and learned patterns of behaviour, to create the play through planning, role formation and allocation and action in the play (Meckley, 1994). For example, Lisa, 5, and Marie, 6, are playing a game of shopping with dolls.

Lisa: I'll be the mum and you can be the grandma.
Marie: No, the aunty, that's better.
Lisa: OK, but I push the pram first ... and you can have this to carry (picks up a doll's car seat and hands it to Marie).
Marie: Well ... we can swap at the shop.
Lisa: And when we get to the shop we'll need money and a list.
Marie: Baby food and nappies, we're right out of nappies.

In this short example, it is clear that Lisa and Marie are creating the role play through a stream of steady verbal and non-verbal communication, determining each role within the game and unfolding the action through negotiation and discussion.

Play can provide children with the opportunity to develop, master and become confident in a range of skills. Although the evidence to support the role of play in the curriculum is inconclusive, there is a general belief (supported by some research), that play helps children with language and social skills, confidence and self-esteem, and in developing and using a wide range of skills and abilities.

3.2 Theories of play

Theorists differ on whether play actually helps children learn new things or whether play has a more significant role in helping children to integrate or consolidate new knowledge into their existing understanding. There is a difference between theories that suggest children are learning new skills and knowledge through play, and those that argue that these are learned through other activities and then practised during play.

Piaget (1962) identified several stages of play linked to his theory of the stages of development. These are:

- **Sensorimotor play** (0–2) – using the senses and motor skills to explore the environment. For example, a baby shaking, mouthing, grasping and throwing a plastic rattle.

- **Imaginative play** (2–7) – role-play, sociodramatic play, fantasy play, self-directed activities. For example, a small group of 4- and 5-year-olds dressing up and acting out the story from a favourite film.

- **Games with rules** (6 upwards) – problem-solving, board games, competitive games and computer games. For example, a 7- and 8-year-old playing cards or a group of 6-, 7- and 8-year-olds playing 'Tiggy'.

Corinne Hutt (1979) identified two types of play, epistemic and ludic. Epistemic play is essentially exploration, finding out about new aspects of the environment. Ludic play is the imaginary, self-directed or 'free-flow' play in which children have the chance to practise new skills and integrate new knowledge. Hutt felt that real learning took place during epistemic play. She did not place as much value on 'free-flow play' as educationalists such as Tina Bruce do. Bruce (1991) argues that free-flow play gives children invaluable opportunities to explore their world, to practise skills, to make sense of their experiences through repetition and to develop co-operative skills such as turn-taking, sharing and planning together. Free-flow play supports language skills in particular as children create and extend play together through discussion and planning.

Some of Vygotsky's (1978) theories about play have already been discussed above. Vygotsky also believed that play has an important role in helping children to understand the function of symbols. During imaginative play, children use objects to represent other things. For example, a child may play 'swords' with a stick or rolled newspaper. The stick or roll is a symbol of a sword. In this way, children become confident in their understanding and use of symbols. You may be wondering why this is so important. Symbols are crucial elements of the world around us. Language, both written and spoken, is symbolic in that we use words, spoken or written, to indicate or represent other things. Vygotsky recognized that the early use of symbols helped children to develop language and literacy skills and to understand and use symbols as part of their own cultural behaviour.

A *chance to think*

Observing play can be a powerful tool in assessing many aspects of a child's development and progress. Play can also give us insights into a child's social skills, the dynamics of the group, language development and emotional issues. In role play or sociodramatic play, children tend to act out themes or roles which are relevant to their own experience or preoccupations. For example, a family of children aged 4, 6 and 7 played 'airports' for weeks after their first experience of travelling by plane. The children used construction skills to build an airport out of bricks and Duplo, and then using small figures, acted out 'checking-in', passport control, boarding, flying and disembarking. The children made sense of their new experiences through re-enactment. They used new language and terminology to plan and discuss the play and to clarify their understanding of the complex and varied processes and stages associated with air travel.

Exercise 2.3

Observe a group of children at play. Record the activities and discussions taking place. Look through your observation notes and answer the following questions:

1. What aspects of development were apparent in the play?

2. What sorts of skills were being shown?

3. What value, if any, did the play have for the children's learning?

   Discuss your findings with a colleague or mentor.

3.3 Supporting play – the adult role

Adults have a range of important roles in supporting children's play. Perhaps the most important issue is for adults to accept and support the role of play in learning and to value play as a medium for learning, not just as a recreational activity or something to fill time after the work is done. The role of learning through play is embedded in the principles of teaching and learning in the *Curriculum Guidance for the Foundation Stage* (QCA, 2000) for 3- to 5-year-olds. This is welcome, not just for the younger children, but because it firmly establishes the role of play in reception classes. However, the role of play is less clear at Key Stage 1 and the ways in which the National Curriculum can be delivered through play are sometimes poorly understood and implemented. Yet we know from our experiences and knowledge of theory that children can learn effectively through both structured and free-flow play, which is effectively supported by skilled adults.

Play has the following features, which are important for learning development:

- Children provide their own high levels of motivation for play.
- Play is often social, developing children's social skills including negotiation, conflict-resolution, sharing, and consideration of others' needs.
- Children learn across subject boundaries through play.
- Children learn in a relaxed and unforced way through play.
- Play is strongly linked to language development.

Intervention in children's play needs to be well considered and based on observation. Some studies show that adults often intervene ineffectively in children's play because they believe their own play ideas are superior to those of the children (Lally, 1989). Such intervention can convey a negative message to children about their own play themes and ideas. It is important to remember that, although children learn a great deal through play, the role of play in learning is an adult interpretation of what play is about. Children play because it is fun to do so, or because they have an idea or experience to explore. Irrelevant adult intervention can result in the play being abandoned.

The debate about the relative value of adult-structured activities and child-directed free-flow play has been explored in depth by theorists such as Bruce (1991) and Moyles (1988). Moyles' 'play spiral' is a useful model to explore of the relationship between structured play, which is usually designed and directed by adults, and free-flow play. In this model, themes from children's free-flow play can be incorporated in the curriculum by building structured activities around them. The structured activities then give children material for their subsequent free-flow play.

The 'play spiral' model attempts to acknowledge the importance of both free-flow and structured activities in learning through play. However, the real issue seems to be the quality of the play experience for the child, regardless of whether it is child or adult directed. Aimless play is as equally unproductive as over-structured activities, which require little input from the child to complete. However, adult intervention, when appropriately used, can both extend the content and duration of play and support children in their play.

For example, the 'airport' game mentioned earlier could have been extended to include airport shopping, buying air tickets and weighing baggage in. The children could have been helped to develop these new themes by suggestions, using a range of props to incorporate them in the game, or an adult joining in the play. All the themes could be developed further to encourage the use of literacy and numeracy skills within the context of the game. With appropriate planning, most play can provide children with educational opportunities, social and practical skills development, and the chance to learn through their own activities.

Adults have a role in helping children with the 'raw material' and the resources for play. Children need first-hand experiences to develop into role play and fantasy play. They also need space, props, possibly playmates, time and ideas. For some children, play is not an easily accessible activity. Adults have a significant role in helping children to learn to play by supporting them and teaching them how to play. Smilansky's work on 'play tutoring' is an example of this. Smilansky (1968) worked with children from disadvantaged environments, training them to role play by playing with them and helping them plan and evaluate their play. The children

showed an increase in the amount of spontaneous role play they involved themselves in and they also showed improvements in cognitive and language development. Although some argued that the children's learning could have been due to
having more adult attention, rather than the play itself, it is important to remember
that not all children know how to play without help.

Children learn play skills and how to communicate about play through playing
with others. Not all children have this opportunity. For some children, access to
play is restricted by their home circumstances, possibly due to lack of resources or
space, or because their parents do not have the time, energy or skills to play with
them. Children may not play because they are ill, or have emotional or behavioural
difficulties, or because they are abused or neglected. Children with disabilities or
learning difficulties may have problems with play because of physical or cognitive
limitations on their access to play. For some children, the social aspects of play may
be difficult, through shyness or lack of confidence or because the child has not
mastered enough skills to play co-operatively with others and to share.

It is clear that adults have an important role in helping children to access play in
a variety of ways. However, it is equally important that they base their intervention
on careful observation of play and that intervention is sensitive and appropriate to
individual children's needs.

Some of the ways in which adults have a role in supporting play include:

• Providing time, space and resources such as play materials.

• Providing first-hand experiences to give children ideas for imaginative play.

• Supporting individual children to access individual and group play.

• Intervening sensitively to extend play by suggesting new themes, providing
  props or resources, or helping to resolve conflicts.

• Communicating about play, planning play with children, discussing and evaluating play and helping children to realize their ideas.

• Being a player.

• Keeping out of play when adult intervention is not needed or wanted.

4. ASPECTS OF THE TEACHING ASSISTANT'S ROLE

The teaching assistant can contribute significantly to all aspects of children's
learning development through both specific activities and through their pastoral
and informal contacts with children. Perhaps one of the most important aspects of
this role is to understand that children are not only learning specific skills and
knowledge, but they are also 'learning to learn'. The process of learning at this
stage of development is as important as the content. Children need to develop the
tools for learning in the long term. Children who have positive experiences of the
learning process will continue to enjoy learning.

Some theorists argue that children who experience formal learning at too early
an age will not develop independent learning habits or real pleasure in learning
(Katz, 1988). There is some debate over whether it is positive in the long run to

have young children in school as early as we do in Britain. Other European countries start children at school at six or even seven and yet they are not relatively behind in literacy and numeracy by secondary school age.

The role of adults in supporting learning and in supporting play has been discussed above. In this section, skills that can be used to support children's learning and development across the curriculum are discussed. Supporting children in specific subject areas is discussed in the relevant chapters.

4.1 Supporting language development

Language development has already been identified as a key tool for shaping and extending cognitive development in young children. Through using and learning new language children give meaning to new aspects of their environment and develop understanding of new experiences. The process of describing what they are doing, sharing ideas and thinking aloud are important parts of the learning process.

Children may be able to use verbal skills when other skills are less developed. Being able to talk, to share ideas and to solve problems verbally may give children a lot of confidence. Children talk most fluently about their own experiences and the things they have actively participated in. For example, Shiraz, 6, had limited reading and writing skills, and was reluctant to talk in class. His confidence was poor and he needed a lot of encouragement to participate in activities. After a holiday abroad in which Shiraz had many new and very different experiences, his support worker suggested he talked to the class for a few minutes about the trip. The few minutes turned into 30 as Shiraz talked confidently and fluently about his experiences and showed various objects to illustrate his talk, and the class listened.

Teaching assistants working with individuals or groups can:

- Explain clearly and with emphasis when modelling a task or activity, breaking it down into a manageable sequence of smaller tasks.

- Listen to children, clarify their ideas and help them to articulate their thoughts.

- Encourage children to talk about their own experiences and unique knowledge.

- Support children and give them time to ask questions and share ideas and thoughts.

- Encourage children to describe their actions or processes to others.

- Support the acquisition of new language through stories, poems, conversation and new experiences.

4.2 Communication skills for working with children

Teaching assistants need to be competent and effective communicators at a range of levels. They spend large parts of their working day communicating with children and adults on a very wide range of issues and subjects. Communication is not only a key skill in the classroom, but it is also important to be able to communicate in different ways for different situations and contexts. Part of the development of professionalism is recognizing and understanding these different contexts and being able to develop and adapt communication skills to meet the requirements of the situation. More general communication skills for teaching assistants will be discussed in Chapter 8, but in this section we will explore the specific skills needed to communicate with children in the classroom and other learning situations.

Communicating with children requires skills in being able to interpret meaning sensitively and appropriately. Children need, above all, to be listened to and responded to in the context of the message they are trying to convey. It is difficult for children to be clear and articulate at times and it is often tempting for busy adults to finish sentences for the child or to interpret what the child is saying before the child has finished saying it. However, children can become discouraged and less enthusiastic if adults do not listen and respond to them properly. Daily conversation is a vital tool in children's learning and development, and yet there is evidence that much of the communication in schools involves adults instructing or questioning children, rather than listening and responding.

Skills for communicating with children include:

- Listening carefully.

- Checking understanding with the child.

- Responding in terms of the child's verbal and non-verbal messages.

- Acknowledging emotions and feelings within the message.

- Avoiding cheerful and bland responses which trivialize the child's message.

- Asking questions which are relevant to the child's message.

- Avoiding questions which are irrelevant to the child's message.

4.3 Developing relationships with children

It is well known that children learn best in an environment where they are respected and warmly treated. However, a study by Elfer (1996) concluded that practitioners working in nurseries did not develop the sort of warm and responsive relationships with children that are crucial to the child's positive learning experience. Children need to feel that they belong and are important within their environment, whatever their economic or social circumstances, family background, culture, religion or level of ability. Yet often adults are too busy or occupied to take time to make supportive relationships with children or to show warmth to them. At worst, children may experience hostility from the adults around them, be shouted at or scapegoated, or labelled as a nuisance or a disruptive force.

Young children need to develop attachments to those who care for them and educate them. It is through these secure foundations that children gain a sense of confidence on which to base their exploration of the world. Clearly, there is a difference between the relationships which children have with parents and other family members, and those they have with staff in schools. However, there are links between the ways that children are treated by the adults around them and aspects of their growth and development.

Bee (2000) identified four dimensions to children's care, which are important in terms of the child's well-being and positive developmental progress. They are:

- warmth

- responsiveness

- control

- communication.

Communication has been discussed above, and the best methods of managing children's behaviour will be discussed in detail in Chapter 7. Warmth and responsiveness are dimensions relating to the level of positive attention you bring to your interactions with children. Warmth involves showing that children are liked and likeable, taking an interest in them and their concerns and responding positively to their communications. Warmth is expressed through our tone of voice, the things we say and our non-verbal communication, such as smiles, eye contact and a pleasant expression. Responsive is partly about responding to children's requests and questions, their immediate concerns and needs, worries and problems. However, it is also about recognizing and responding to non-verbal communications which the child is not expressing openly – a sad face, avoidance of other children, unexplained tears, an anxious expression. It is about knowing children, anticipating their needs and recognizing when the child is unhappy or has a problem.

A chance to think

The teaching assistant has an important role in developing supportive relationships with the children in their care. You need to be able to show warmth, within the boundaries of a professional role, and to respect the child's ideas, views and opinions. Children should not be shouted at or treated with disrespect. They should be listened to and responded to in a warm and friendly way, acknowledging their immaturity and lack of knowledge in many areas. Anyone working with children needs to have a genuine liking for and interest in them, and to recognize their needs and how to respond to these. For some children, school is a scary place, and adults need to be sensitive to this. Schools have some very young pupils who may, at first, find the school environment harsh and difficult to comprehend. Children learn best in an environment in which they are confident and supported by the adults around them.

Exercise 2.4

Look at the list of dimensions to children's care discussed above. Make a note of examples from your own practice that demonstrate your warmth and responsiveness to children. Consider whether you could have responded differently in other situations, to better meet the child's needs. Discuss your notes with a colleague or mentor.

4.4 Differentiating learning activities

One of the greatest challenges within your role can be working with groups or individual children where there is a need to differentiate the activity to meet the needs of children at different developmental stages and different levels of aptitude in their learning. Differentiation is the process by which planned activities are varied to meet the needs of a range of children. Differentiation is a crucial aspect of teaching and learning in classes of up to 30 children, where there may be a wide range of ability. Some differences in ability will be based on intellectual capacity, some on developmental stage, which can vary significantly in young children, and some on more temporary factors influencing individual children, such as problems or changes at home, bullying at school or illness. All differentiation should be based on careful assessment of children's learning needs and abilities.

Bentley *et al.* (1999: 46) identifies categories of children who may need differentiated work:

- Children who display challenging and distracting behaviour.

- Children who are 'invisible'.

- Children for whom English is an additional language.

- Children who have learning difficulties.

- Children who have physical challenges.

- Children who are very able.

O'Hara (2000: 69) discusses various types of differentiation:

- By support.

- By outcome and task.

Differentiation by support refers to the extent to which the child or children work independently or with help. You may be asked to work on a whole class activity with particular children who are less confident about tackling tasks independently or who may need additional explanation of the requirements of the task. It is important to maximize the extent to which each child works independently, while not leaving them to struggle. Using encouragement and praise and good levels of communication will help the child to work as autonomously as possible.

Differentiation by outcome is where all children work at their own level on the same task, but the outcome varies between children. Differentiation by task is where children may be learning the same content through different types of activities or at different levels or with different methods of support. Part of your work may be to develop activities set by the teacher to meet the needs of particular children. This may involve simplifying the task or changing it. It may involve looking at the overall learning outcomes and recognizing that some children may need to go back a few stages to consolidate their learning of basic principles. It is very important that decisions about differentiating work should be part of the teamwork approach between yourself and the teacher. The teacher has responsibility to ensure all learning activities are accessible to all children, but your feedback on children's ability and performance is crucial to accurate assessment of these factors.

A chance to think

Differentiation is very important in meeting varying needs within a class. However, in order to be effective a number of issues need to be considered. These include an assessment of the child or children's specific needs; the best form of differentiation to meet these needs; the materials or resources needed to vary activities or create new activities; how the learning outcomes can best be met and how the outcomes can be evaluated.

Exercise 2.5

Working with a teacher, identify a group or individual child who needs differentiated work for a planned activity. Plan differentiated work for the child or group, taking into account:

1. The child or children's needs.

2. Required resources.

3. The planned learning outcomes.

4. How the outcomes can be evaluated.

Discuss your plans with the teacher and evaluate the outcomes of the activity.

4.5 Supporting children with special educational needs (SEN)

There is a danger in labelling children as having special educational needs (SEN), in that it may lead us to assume that these children are all the same, with the same needs and same difficulties in accessing the curriculum. Children with SEN learn through the same processes and practices as other children. Their different needs depend on the unique features of the individual child, which must be identified and responded to in order to best meet that child's needs. The important issues to remember are that to support children with SEN effectively we need to understand the child's level of ability and developmental stage and know the focus and detail of the child's Individual Education Plan (IEP). Roffey (1999: 78) suggests that in order to support a child with SEN the following areas need to be assessed:

- Physical needs

- Self-help needs

- Communication needs

- Hearing needs

- Visual needs

- General learning needs

- Emotional social and behavioural needs

- Medical needs.

The role of the teaching assistant can be crucial in supporting children with SEN. As well as establishing a good relationship with the child, you need to know:

- How your work with the child supports her progress towards the targets within her IEP.

- The teaching and learning styles which best meet the child's needs.

- How to communicate most effectively with him/her.

- How your work with the individual child fits in to the whole class work.

These issues should be resolved in consultation with the class teacher and Special Educational Needs Co-ordinator (SENCO). If you regularly support a particular child with SEN, it is good practice to ensure that you attend the child's review meetings, and that you are part of the assessment and planning process for the child.

CONCLUSIONS

It is important to acknowledge that there are different approaches to teaching and learning in the early years. In this chapter, the factors which contribute to a positive learning environment for young children have been discussed, along with theories which have influenced how we approach teaching and learning in schools. The different views on how children learn best have been discussed and some of the tensions between different approaches identified. The role of play in learning has been examined in terms of the different stages of the curriculum. Key factors in supporting children's learning have been explored in terms of the teaching assistant's role, including building good relationships with children based on high levels of effective communication, warmth and responsiveness. Strategies for supporting children with specific needs have been discussed in terms of the teaching assistant's role.

NOTES FOR FURTHER READING

Bee, H. (2000)
The Developing Child 9th edn.
Needham Heights, MA: Allyn and Bacon.

Bennett, N., Wood, L. and Rodger, S. (1997)
Teaching through Play.
Milton Keynes: Open University Press.

Bentley, D., Chamberlin, R., Gray, D., Lynch, M., Burman, C., Clipson-Boyles, S., Holderness, J. and Reid, D. (1999)
The Really Practical Guide to English.
Cheltenham: Nelson Thornes.

Bronfenbrenner, U. (1979)
The Ecology of Human Development.
Cambridge, MA: Harvard University Press.

Bruce, T. (1991)
Time to Play in Early Childhood Education.
London: Hodder and Stoughton.

Bruner, J. S. (1966)
Towards a Theory of Instruction.
Cambridge, MA: Harvard University Press.

Bruner, J. S. (1983)
Child's Talk: Learning to Use Language.
New York: W. W. Norton and Co.

Donaldson, M. (1978)
Children's Minds.
Glasgow: Fontana.

Elfer, P. (1996)
'Building Intimacy in relationships with young children in nurseries'.
Early Years, Vol. 16.

Hurst, V. and Joseph, J. (1998)
Supporting Early Learning.
Milton Keynes: Open University Press.

Hutt, C. (1979)
'Play in the under-5s; form, development and function' in Howells, J. G. (ed.)
Modern Perspectives in the Psychiatry of Infancy.
New York: Brunner/Marcel.

Katz, L. (1988)
'What should young children be learning?'
American Educator, Summer.

Lally, M. (1989)
An Integrated Approach to the National Curriculum in the Early Years.
London: NCB.

Meckley, A. (1994)
'Play, communication and cognition'.
Communication and Cognition, 27 (3).

Merry, R. (1998)
Successful Children, Successful Teaching.
Milton Keynes: Open University Press.

Moyles, J. R. (1988)
Just Playing? – The Role and Status of Play in Early Childhood.
Milton Keynes: Open University Press.

Moyles, J. R. (ed.) (1994)
The Excellence of Play.
Milton Keynes: Open University Press.

O'Hara, M. (2000)
Teaching 3–8.
London: Continuum.

Piaget, J. (1962)
Play, Dreams and Imitation in Childhood.
London: Routledge and Kegan Paul.

Qualifications and Curriculum Authority (QCA) (2000)
Sudbury: QCA.
Curriculum Guidance for the Foundation Stage.

Roffey, S. (1999)
Special Needs in the Early Years – Collaboration, Communication and Co-ordination.
London: David Fulton.

Smilansky, S. (1968)
The Effects of Socio-Dramatic Play on Disadvantaged Preschool Children.
New York: John Wiley.

Tizard, B. and Hughes, M. (1984)
Young Children Learning: Talking and Thinking at Home and at School.
London: Fontana.

Vygotsky, L. (1978)
Mind in Society.
Cambridge, MA: Harvard University Press.

Wood, D. J., Bruner, J. S. and Ross, G. (1976)
The role of tutoring in problem-solving.
Journal of Child Psychology and Psychiatry, 17, 89–100.

CHAPTER 3

Supporting Key Stage 1 English

INTRODUCTION

Developing language and literacy is central to the early years curriculum, providing a basis for subsequent learning development. Within the National Curriculum, English is one of the three core subjects, but it is often viewed as the most important subject of all. English language and literacy is not only a subject in itself, but the medium through which children can access all other subjects within the curriculum. The importance of language development as a basis for the rest of a child's learning development has been discussed in Chapter 2. English is, therefore, taught and learned not only as a discrete subject, but also as a subject embedded within the curriculum as a whole.

The National Literacy Strategy (NLS) was introduced in 1998 as a method of raising standards and providing a more coherent approach to all teaching and learning of literacy. The *Framework for Teaching* (DfEE, 1998) prescribes what is taught and how it is taught, and there is an emphasis on whole class teaching as well as individual and small group activities within the literacy hour. A range of support materials for the National Literacy Strategy was introduced in 2000/1 (see References and Notes for further reading at the end of the chapter).

Concerns have been expressed about whether the prescriptive nature of the strategy would stifle good teaching and limit the learning opportunities for children within the literacy hour. Other concerns centred on whether the approach of the strategy is compatible with how young children learn best. However, the National Literacy Strategy also emphasizes oral work, interaction between children and teacher and group and individual work, as part of the literacy hour.

In reading this chapter you will come across a number of terms that are regularly used in schools and in literature relating to the development of early literacy. The meanings of theses terms are discussed in the text, but you can also use the Glossary for more detailed definitions.

Supporting literacy development

McNaughton (1995) identifies three ways, described as 'tutorial configurations', in which children can be supported in their literacy development as part of their everyday activities. These are:

1. Collaborative participation – the child works with a more expert person, gradually becoming more independent.

2. Directed performance – the expert models the activity and the child copies what is modelled.

3. Item conveyancing – the child gains information by asking the more expert person and responding to the reply.

In many situations these different strategies are all used at different times, in response to the needs of the child and the context of the literacy activity. Much of the work of teaching assistants in primary schools is focused on supporting children in the acquisition of literacy skills, through talking and listening to children, reading with them and listening to them read, supporting children's writing and language development and involving children in activities which will extend their understanding of the role of literacy in their everyday lives. Teaching assistants often have a role in literacy hour, supporting individual or groups of children to understand and access the learning that is taking place. The teaching assistant's role and responsibilities are defined by the curriculum planning within the class and identified aims and objectives for each session. As always, the teaching assistant's specific role in a particular session is agreed with the class teacher in order to achieve these objectives.

1. LEARNING ABOUT LITERACY AT HOME

It is important to remember that children have many experiences of literacy before they arrive in school. These experiences and how they relate to teaching and learning within Key Stage 1 are important determinants of how the child accesses the English curriculum. There are many factors that influence children's early experience of literacy, many of them rooted in the role of literacy in the child's particular culture. Sociocultural theories of literacy emerged in the 1990s, based on the view that there are many different types of literacy and ways of approaching literacy, depending on the social and cultural context (Barratt-Pugh, 2000a: 4).

Children learn a great deal about literacy within their families, and bring this understanding with them when they enter more formal learning situations. As such, the individual children in a group starting Key Stage 1 will have a very varied understanding of literacy and a range of different literacy skills.

Children can learn many things about literacy from observing and participating in literacy activities within day-to-day family life. For example, children can learn the uses of writing through making shopping lists, writing notes and messages, writing letters and cards, and signing names. Children can learn about the uses of reading through watching others and participating in reading newspapers and magazines or using the internet to gather information; though reading letters and notes; through reading environmental information like posters, shop signs or road information. In this way, children learn about the importance of literacy and what it is for. They also learn about how literacy 'works' in their own particular cultural environment. This is not the same range of experiences for all children. For example, in one household a child may learn a lot about literacy through the use of a computer. In another household, a child may make up and write stories as a pastime, gradually developing the skills to record these.

The many and varied things that young children have learned about literacy are often reflected through their play. Children demonstrate through role play and sociodramatic play that they understand the uses of literacy. In play, children show that they understand the uses of print in a wide range of contexts, such as giving and receiving messages, making lists, sending greetings, directions, labels and signs. For example, Fazan and Gemma, both four, are playing 'shops' at home. They have set out their stall with various items for sale on it. They have made 'labels' with 'prices' and a 'sign' for the shop. They have put 'notices' up in the shop with special offers. They have made 'shopping lists' for the customers to use. There is little about the use of literacy in this context that they do not yet know about.

A chance to think

We know that children's understanding and use of literacy is rooted in their culture and the way literacy is viewed and applied in their home and community. Children come to school with their own unique knowledge of literacy, which will shape their approach to and success with more formal learning of literacy. Children initially learn about literacy through increasing involvement in literacy activities within the family. This will vary considerably between children, reflecting the use of literacy in their family environment.

Exercise 3.1

Ask two different children about their understanding of the uses of literacy outside school. What sort of uses do they and their family have for reading? Why do they write and what do they write about? Record and compare the children's responses. Are they the same or similar or quite different? Discuss your findings with a colleague or mentor.

The challenge for adults supporting children with literacy development is to understand that an individual child's knowledge and understanding of literacy may vary a great deal from the next child's and to develop a flexible range of responses to children's needs in this area. For some children, the literacy they have learned at home will be quite different to literacy in school, meaning that children from different social and economic backgrounds have unequal access to the literacy curriculum in school. Understanding how and what children have already learned about literacy can be important in providing the most useful support and learning activities to help a particular child.

Children not only have different experiences of literacy within the home, but many will speak with different accents, and use different grammar and vocabulary to standard English. Although children benefit from learning to use standard English, particularly in written work, it is important to acknowledge the child's local dialect as a valid language and not belittle it or imply that it is inferior in some way. For some children, English is a second language and the child may need support developing their use of English. It is important to value the child's multilingual ability as well as recognizing the difficulties the child may experience in grasping the curriculum if their English is undeveloped. Barratt-Pugh (2000b: 174) suggests that developing home languages and literacies is needed to:

- Maintain family and community relationships.
- Develop in children a positive sense of identity.
- Enable children to reach their full potential.
- Enable children to use their linguistic skills as a means of potential employment.

In order to function well in an increasingly complex society, children need to develop a range of complex and varied literacy skills. Bentley *et al.* (1999: 6) suggest that children need to be 'TV literate, computer literate, advertising literate and book literate'. The need for high standards across a range of different types of literacy reflects current social and cultural norms, and teaching and learning of English should reflect this.

For some children opportunities to develop literacy within the home may be limited due to social and economic factors. There may be few books, or children may not see parents reading or writing in their daily lives. Experience of the wider world may be limited, giving children few chances to develop their understanding of the role of literacy in our day-to-day lives, through access to environmental print. For example, Adam, at the age of three, had few first-hand experiences outside his own home because access to such experiences had been limited by mental health problems and poor economic circumstances in his family. He had never been on holiday or a day trip, nor travelled any distance from his immediate community. There were no books in the home and his carers did not read. Conversation was generally limited to instructions and admonishments. As a result, until he attended nursery, Adam had not discovered much about the uses of literacy at all.

It is important for children who have had limited access to print to have the opportunity to immerse themselves in a print-rich environment. Joe, who was a reluctant reader and who showed little interest in stories or poems, was encouraged to read by carers who filled his home with the spoken and written word. Strategies adopted by his carers included reading interesting articles from papers out loud, talking about books they had read, emphasizing the use of text by reading out operating instructions for toys, TV and radio guides and recipes. Gradually, Joe began to recognize the various uses of literacy and to develop an interest in building up his own literacy skills.

2. | LITERACY IN THE FOUNDATION STAGE – 3 TO 5 YEARS

Within the *Curriculum Guidance for the Foundation Stage* (see Chapter 2), there is an emphasis on language development through 'conversation, open-ended questions and thinking out loud' (QCA, 2000: 23). Working towards the Early Learning Goal of 'communication, language and literacy' gives children the opportunity to be involved in activities that are enjoyable in their own right, but which also contribute to the development of literacy skills. These include opportunities for discussion and conversation, reading with and to children, sharing songs and rhymes, poems and stories, and immersing children in a literacy-rich environment. There is a strong emphasis on a multi-sensory approach and learning through play.

Children are supported in activities which give them a chance to communicate with adults and other children and to develop and practice skills through play and conversation.

One of the aims of the Foundation Stage is to build on learning which has taken place in the home through structured activities and play, which reflect the informal ways in which young children learn, their diverse levels of development and individual needs. Bentley *et al.* (1999: 12) comment that classrooms for the under-fives should be full of print of different types and purposes 'in the form of signs, labels, packages, lists and notices'. These give children the opportunity to learn what print is for, in terms of communications, and also to use the content of the message in their activities and play.

In the Foundation Stage, children are taught through more informal methods and there is an emphasis on experiential learning and an integrated curriculum. For example, children at a nursery school developed a topic on pets. They looked at books about different types of pets and talked about their habits and care needs. They drew different types of pets and modelled them. Finally, they walked in two groups to the local pet shop. The first group bought a tank and ornaments. The second group bought a goldfish and food. This topic gave the children the opportunity to recognize the use of books for reference; to talk about the type of information required in order to choose a pet and to access sources of this infor-mation; to look at print in the environment, such as writing on the fish food packet and labels and notices in the pet shop; and to use their learning to complete the successful purchase of a pet. In addition, the children were delighted with the topic and with the fish. Their sense of 'ownership' of the activities and their growing sense of responsibility contributed to positive self-confidence and good self-esteem.

Children can develop their understanding of the role of literacy in their lives and the lives of others by observing how adults use literacy skills in their daily activities. The main targets for effective learning are:

- opportunities to speak and listen and represent ideas in their activities.

- using communication, language and literacy in every part of the curriculum.

- being immersed in an environment rich in print and possibilities for communica-tion.

(QCA, 2000: 45)

Adults can support progress towards these targets by:

- Talking and listening to children, making time for them to express their ideas and thoughts.

- Reading to children from a wide range of texts and environmental print.

- Choosing stories, poems, and non-fiction with children.

- Telling nursery rhymes, discussing and identifying rhyming words, playing at making up silly rhymes.

- Alliteration games such as 'Ernie the elephant elegantly elbowed the egg ... ', adding on as many words as the children can think of.

- Talking and sharing ideas about different forms of print and how they contribute to our daily activities.

- Writing for children or sharing the process of writing with children, as part of activities and games.

- Discussing the child's interpretation of the marks she makes on paper.

- Sharing messages with children and discussing the usefulness of writing.

- Encouraging the use of literacy skills in role play or sociodramatic play, such as making 'shopping lists' or writing 'messages' or 'notices'.

- Developing understanding of the uses of literacy through structured activities, such as using reference books to support a topic.

A chance to think

The ways in which children learn in the Foundation Stage can be quite different to the types of learning and teaching at Key Stage 1. Children have to adapt to a more formal style of learning and a subject-based curriculum in their transition from reception class to Year 1. There is less learning through play and more teacher-led activities. For example, the literacy hour involves more formal instruction and whole class teaching than many young children may yet be used to. For many children, this will be a welcome opportunity to extend and build on existing skills and to develop their knowledge further. They will have the maturity to access the curriculum and enjoy their learning within it. However, developmental levels vary greatly between young children, and for some, the change in approach may be difficult to adjust to.

Exercise 3.2

Read the case study and answer the following questions.

Anna

Anna is one of the younger children in Year 1. The teacher has noticed that Anna is not concentrating well during the whole class teaching during the literacy hour, and that she is reluctant to tackle the individual and small group work independently. Anna's progress has been slow in the two months she has been in Year 1, and she does not always seem to know what is expected of her. The teacher has asked you to support Anna during the literacy hour.

1. What sort of approach would you take to supporting Anna?

2. What type of skills would you need for this approach to be effective?

Compare your answers with the suggestions on page 163.

3. KEY STAGE 1 ENGLISH

Guidance as to how and what should be taught to develop literacy and language at Key Stage 1 is found in the National Curriculum for England (DfEE, 2000), and in the *National Literacy Strategy: Framework for Teaching* (DfEE, 1998). A number of volumes of support materials and guidance have been published to accompany the National Literacy Strategy and to use within the literacy hour. These include whole-class teaching materials such as the *National Literacy Strategy: Progression in Phonics* (DfEE, 2000a) and the *National Literacy Strategy: Developing Early Writing* (DfEE, 2001). There are three areas of knowledge, skills and understanding for English within the National Curriculum at Key Stage 1:

- speaking and listening

- reading

- writing.

The guidance emphasizes the need to integrate the separate skills but also to give them equal weighting. As such, the areas of study are not taught separately but are integrated through the same activities.

4. SPEAKING AND LISTENING

The ability to use spoken language effectively is probably one of the most important skills developed at Key Stage 1. 'Oracy', as speaking and listening is sometimes described, is a central skill for learning and for life. The process of acquiring a wide range of language skills is closely linked to the development of thinking and understanding, predicting, theorizing and reasoning. Children need to learn that there is more than one form of language, and, as described above, these forms have value in different contexts. For example, a child may use familiar speech forms in her home and community, but may need to use other types of language forms at school and in the wider world.

Speaking and listening in the home and pre-school contexts is encouraged through conversation and discussion, planning together and reflecting on activities or ideas. For example, a child who is baking with a carer at home may plan the activity with the adult, discussing ingredients, methods, possible outcomes and pitfalls. He may then discuss the processes of baking at each stage of the activity, and then reflect on how well the activity went and the quality of the outcomes. The child will have the opportunity to plan, predict, reason and reflect.

Play is one of the most significant media for language development in the early years, as discussed in Chapter 2. Through play, young children practise new vocabulary, develop new concepts and ideas, and share language with each other. Vygotsky (1978) theorized that children develop language through play and that this process is closely linked to cognitive development. A great deal of skill development takes place during play as children discuss choices, negotiate play themes, practise vocabulary, develop characters and story lines, resolve conflicts and share ideas. For example, Brian, five, and Dave, seven, are playing in the playground at lunchtime. All week they have played a game they call 'Dinosaurs' using characters from films they have seen as a starting point, developing play themes and story lines through discussion, sharing ideas and concepts, choosing from a range of possible ideas, negotiating differences of opinion and evaluating the quality of the play.

When children enter school they are speaking and listening in quite a different context. There are fewer opportunities for one-to-one conversations than at home or in pre-school settings, and more rules about when children can speak and what they are expected to speak about. Supporting children to learn about taking turns, listening for longer periods and being spoken to in a larger group rather than as an individual, is an important part of the role of the adult.

4.1 Developing speaking and listening

The teaching assistant's role in supporting speaking and listening is varied depending on whether you are working with individuals or groups. However, there are some basic principles that you need to consider in any context in which children are being supported with speaking and listening. They are:

- Modelling and encouraging good practice in listening.
- Modelling and encouraging effective use of spoken language.
- Using and encouraging different types of language effectively.
- Developing understanding of different types of English and other languages.
- Valuing the child's use of language and listening skills.

Looking at these more closely can give us some ideas of the skills you need to develop or extend to work with children on the speaking and listening requirements of Key Stage 1.

4.2 Good practice in listening

Key skills for listening at Key Stage 1 are:

- attention
- concentration
- appropriate response
- effective response
- asking appropriate questions based on what is being heard
- remembering
- taking different views into account.

It is important for adults working with young children to model these skills as part of their support strategy. It is very easy to not really listen to children as we plan our next task and think ahead in a busy day. Children can be acutely aware that you are not paying attention! So, how do we make it clear that we are paying attention and concentrating on what the child is saying, responding appropriately and valuing what they say? Important factors include:

- Making eye contact and using non-verbal signals such as smiles, nods and gestures to indicate understanding.

- Responding with relevant comments, questions or answers.

- Listening to the underlying message which the child may have difficulty expressing verbally, but which may be apparent in the child's non-verbal signals.

- Bringing knowledge of the child and the context in which they are speaking to bear on our response e.g. acknowledging the difficulties of speaking in English as a second language.

- Remembering relevant points from previous discussions.

Some of the things which indicate that adults are not listening attentively include:

- Doing something else at the same time, looking away or being poised to move away.

- Making bland, irrelevant noises or comments.

- Interrupting, finishing the child's sentences or finding words for the child.

- Assuming you know what the child is saying before he/she has finished speaking.

- Failing to recognize the underlying message.

- Not making time to listen.

Modelling good practice in listening is important in helping children to develop their own listening skills. Other strategies for supporting the development of listening skills include:

- Using open questions to check that listening has taken place e.g. 'What happened after that?'

- Checking the child's understanding of what has been said through discussion.

- Setting tasks which rely on the child having paid attention.

- Encouraging the child to ask questions about what has been said.

- Encouraging groups of children to share their differing perceptions of the topic or issue under discussion.

A chance to think

Listening is probably the most important communication skill of all, but despite this, many adults and children have not sufficiently developed this skill. Listening carefully and attentively can lead to a better level of comprehension and a clearer concept of the issue under discussion. Children who have difficulty in listening can miss out on understanding, deeper meanings, areas of knowledge and instructions. In order to help children to develop listening skills, adults need to create an environment in which listening can take place effectively, as well as modelling good listening skills themselves.

Exercise 3.3

Write two lists, one of factors that could inhibit development of listening skills and one of factors that could support the development of listening skills, in a Year 1 literacy hour. How could you contribute to encouraging listening skills among the children you work with? Discuss your ideas with a mentor and compare them with the sample answers on page 164.

4.3   Effective use of spoken language

Children model their use of language on both adults and peers, rapidly accommodating new vocabulary and modes of speech into their repertoire. The ways in which the adults around them use language is crucial in determining how well children learn to speak and use spoken language. It is important to recognize that the benefits of talking with children are not confined to the classroom, but are included in all the opportunities you make to converse with them.

Effective use of spoken language is based on listening. Your responses to the child and the development of conversations with a child should be dependent on careful listening to their side of the conversation. Children need to develop confidence in speaking and the use of language. They can be encouraged to do this through appropriate and sensitive responses, which indicate that you have listened to the child. Children gain confidence when they realize that their contributions are valued and influential in the conversation.

Speaking is not a single purpose activity. We speak for a multitude of different purposes, using a range of different styles relevant to the context. The types of talk which children need to develop at Key Stage 1 are:

- storytelling
- imaginative play and drama
- reading aloud
- reciting poetry and nursery rhymes
- exploring ideas
- developing ideas
- clarifying ideas
- predicting outcomes
- discussing possibilities
- describing events
- describing observations
- describing experiences
- explaining choices

- giving reasons for opinions

- giving reasons for actions.

The curriculum should include a range of activities through which the children can develop different types of talk for different purposes.

4.4 Supporting speaking

Your role should include modelling appropriate talk for different contexts. For example, giving children examples of explaining, describing and discussing within your work with them. It is important to use the words to describe the type of talk you are involved in, such as 'I am explaining' or 'Can you describe?' so that the children learn more about the different uses of the various types of talk.

Children often make mistakes in grammar when they are talking. Correcting children's use of words or grammatical faults is less helpful than repeating back the 'right' word, without comment on the child's use of language. For example, if a child says, 'I runned down the street' it is more helpful to reply, 'You ran down the street, did you?' than, 'You don't say runned, you say ran.' Often children will apply the rules of English language in a logical way only to find that one of the many exceptions to the rule has wrong-footed them. It can be frustrating for children to be corrected all the time. However, children need repetition to aid their retention of language, so it is important to ensure that different types of language are used repeatedly in appropriate contexts.

Strategies for encouraging different types of talk:

- Asking open-ended questions (questions which require a sentence as an answer, not just 'yes' or 'no').

- Asking children their views and opinions.

- Encouraging children to ask questions.

- Asking for suggestions about how to organize displays or any other aspect of the classroom.

- Sharing informal conversations e.g. about pets, friends, favourite TV programmes, hobbies.

Children who are not confident about speaking need to be encouraged to talk about familiar things to do with family and home life. It may be better to encourage reluctant talkers to speak in smaller groups or individually. Asking questions where you know the child has the answer can help the child to gain confidence to speak out.

4.5 Multi-lingual and bilingual children

Children who are multi-lingual or bilingual need to be immersed in the spoken English language with many opportunities to listen and practise vocabulary and sentence construction. They need a highly supportive environment, based on respect for their first language and acknowledgement that they are not only learning a further language, but also using that language to learn other things. It may be worth remembering that functioning in an educational setting while using a second language is something that most adults would find a major challenge!

Multi-lingual children who are well supported should have many opportunities to:

- Talk and listen in groups.

- Ask and answer questions.

- Be supported by their peers.

- Seek clarification about instructions or activities.

- Have their first language acknowledged and recognized.

- Have their ability to function in more than one language recognized as a positive skill and not a problem.

In addition, multi-lingual children may well come from a wide range of different cultural and social backgrounds. O'Hara (2000: 23) points out that it is important not to treat them as a homogeneous group. Classroom displays and resources should reflect a wide range of local cultures, dual language books and tapes should be available, and displays should reflect and celebrate cultural diversity. However, it is important to represent the range of cultures in a non-stereotypical way. It will only confuse children and create stereotypes if particular cultures are presented in ways that are not typical of families within the school. Not all British-Asian mothers wear traditional dress, so always depicting them in saris or shalwar kameez (trousers and long top) may result in bafflement!

4.6 Resources for supporting speaking and listening

So, what do we talk about with children? And how do we help them talk in ways which extend and develop their use of different types of language? We all know that some approaches to talking with children can be distinctly unfruitful. For example, any parent who has asked the question, 'What did you do at school today?' probably knows that there is a good chance that the answer will be, 'I don't know'. Asking the right type of questions and using appropriate stimuli to encourage different types of talk is an important part of developing oracy. Bentley *et al.* (1999) describe three sorts of resources for supporting children to structure talk. These are:

- Stimulus resources such as photographs, stories, poems, videos.

- Support resources such as instruction sheets, clue cards, clocks.

- Goal resources such as charts, lists, pictures, graphs.

(Adapted from Bentley *et al.*, 1999: 69 Fig. 7.6)

Stimulus resources are a starting point for talk, giving children a focus for speaking. For example, children in a reception class took photos of themselves as babies or toddlers as a topic. They discussed the context of the photos, talked about who had taken the photo, and what they were doing in the photo as part of the topic. In this way, the photos acted as a stimulus to describing events and experiences. Support resources are those that provide a framework for an activity, such as an instruction sheet used to give guidelines. Finally, a goal resource is one which relates to the outcomes of the talk, for example, using a score chart to record differences in hair and eye colour as part of a group discussion on diversity.

A *chance to think*

The different uses of language have to be learned by children through practice across a range of activities and contexts. This practice takes place across the whole curriculum. For example, children may 'describe' as part of the literacy hour, in response to requests such as, 'Describe what happened next in the story' or questions such as, 'Can you describe what X was wearing/doing/saying/planning/thinking in the story?'.

However, children also develop and use their skills to describe in science, geography, history and other subjects. For example, the children in a Year 1 class were doing a science experiment, which involved putting white flowers in water containing different coloured food dyes. The stem of one flower was split lengthwise and half placed in green-coloured water and half in red-coloured water. The children were asked to describe the changes in the colour of the different flowers after a few days. They were also asked to discuss the possible outcomes of the experiment and predict what might happen before the experiment was started; to explain what might have happened to change the colour of the flowers and to give reasons for their explanations; and to discuss further experiments they could do to confirm their findings.

In a single activity, children had the opportunity to use a range of the different types of talk developed in Key Stage 1.

Exercise 3.4

Look at the list of different types of talk developed at Key Stage 1 above and give examples, from your own experience, of the opportunities Key Stage 1 children in your school have had to use these in the last few weeks. Which activities gave the children the widest range of opportunities to develop different types of talk? Were there any missed opportunities where talk could have been developed further? What was your own role and could it have been expanded on to support the children in developing their talk further?

Share your ideas with a colleague or mentor and check their ideas about how to extend activities to include more types of talk.

---

5. | READING

The process of determining the best way of teaching and learning reading has been controversial, involving an ongoing debate about 'best methods' and a long history of changing approaches. The debate has been divided between methods which focus on teaching children sounds and letters, and methods which focus on children learning to recognize words as a whole within text. Currently, best practice draws from across the range of these approaches, combining aspects of different methods to give children a number of strategies for tackling texts.

The *National Literacy Strategy: Progression in Phonics* 'stresses the importance of teaching children to tackle texts from both ends, from the text 'down', so to speak, and from sounds and spellings 'up''. (DfEE, 2000a).

There are a number of different strands to developing literacy, many of them rooted in the early years and pre-school experiences. Bentley *et al.* (1999: 7) states that 'to become literate, children need:

- pre-reading stories and rhymes

- early intervention for those who make a slow start

- interesting, meaningful texts

- phonic instruction

- enthusiastic teachers

- interested and involved parents who read to their children regularly

- personal involvement

- lots of practice'.

5.1 Stages of learning to read

Learning to read is not a single activity, as we have already discovered. There are a range of skills and aptitudes which children develop through infancy and onwards which contribute to their ultimate ability to learn to read. Some of these relate to learning in the home and pre-school as discussed above. Children go through several stages of learning to read, starting from pre-school onwards:

1. As children start to recognize and understand the relevance of environmental print they may learn to say familiar words from their shape and location e.g. the author's children all knew TESCO at an early age.

2. In the early alphabetical stage children use some sound-letter links, often initial sounds, to read some words. They add these skills to the growing number of words they recognize by sight.

3. In the later alphabetical stage children learn to 'sound out' words (segment) and then blend them, so they have a much greater number of words they know by sight, and a greater skill in reading new words.

4. In the final stage, children become confident readers using a range of skills to tackle unfamiliar text and reading and enjoying a range of books.

It is important to remember that children develop reading skills at widely varying rates. Although early detection of reading problems is important, they should not be based on a rigid view of where children should have progressed to by certain dates in the calendar. There are many different rates of overall development for young children and the differences between youngest and oldest children in a class can be very noticeable in Key Stage 1. For example, the author observed a group of six Year 2 pupils reading silently in the first week of term. The oldest girl, aged 7 that month, was reading *Harry Potter* with confidence and skill. The youngest boy, who had had his sixth birthday during the previous month, was struggling with one of the middle stages of the *Oxford Reading Tree*. The other children were all at different levels of ability somewhere between these two.

Rohl (2000) comments that differences in progress can be linked not just to cognitive ability but to environmental factors which can include the experiences the child has had pre-school and the types of literacy which are used in the home. Problems may reflect social and economic factors that influence the child's social and emotional development. They may also reflect more specific learning delays or difficulties in some children.

5.2 The different approaches to teaching and learning reading

Current approaches to teaching and learning reading include the most effective aspects of different methods developed and discarded over the years. Within the National Literacy Strategy these include bringing the following 'searchlights' to bear on the text:

- phonics (sounds and spelling)
- grammatical knowledge
- knowledge of context
- word recognition and graphic knowledge.

Children use some or all of these strategies to make sense of the text, breaking down words into separate sounds and then blending them, using the context and their knowledge of grammar to give clues to the meaning of the word and using recognition of some words to support understanding of the whole. However, as well as the acquisition of technical skills children have to want to read, because they have learned to understand and enjoy stories. Children should be read aloud to throughout early and late infancy, the Foundation Stage, Key Stage 1 and beyond. Children learn many things from being read to:

- to enjoy fiction and non-fiction, poems and rhymes.
- how stories 'work' in terms of the beginning, middle and end.
- how stories link to their own experiences.
- how print determines a story each time and the link between the spoken and written word.
- how to be imaginative and creative in making their own stories.

Bielby (1998) argues that in a balanced approach to learning reading, the child uses three sources of information:

- the grammatical context – what she knows about how words and sentences fit together.
- the meaning context – what she perceives as a likely probable meaning as she progresses through the text.
- the text – the printed words on the page.

(Bielby, 1998: 11)

Within this balanced approach, children learn about different strategies concurrently. For example, children can start to tackle text at the same time as learning phonetic skills, rather than learning these in a strict order. Children will use a range of cues to determine what the text means, including:

- What will probably come next in the context of the meaning of the text?

- What will probably come next in the context of what the child knows about grammar?

- What the text actually says.

- The action in, or content of, the pictures.

The child will use these cues simultaneously to determine meaning by a process of cross-checking. Bielby (1998: 13) describes this process as follows:

> At its best the interaction between the sources of information operates in the following way: decoding the print takes the leading role, but may be supported where the context of meaning primes the reader's expectancy, facilitating both word identification and comprehension. The overall coherence of grammar and meaning confirm the reading, and the reading extends the overall meaning.

However, children can become over-dependent on context and grammatical knowledge to 'read' text which is well known to them and which is designed to be predictable. Although this can build up confidence in that the child is successfully reading real text, it may not equip the child for tackling more difficult, unfamiliar words or texts. Children also need to develop strategies to decode individual words from their sounds and spellings as a way of progressing to reading more complex text with fewer clues within it (text without many illustrations, for example). This is described as the development of phonological awareness.

6. KEY SKILLS FOR READING AT KEY STAGE 1

Phonological awareness

Phonological awareness is the ability to understand the different sounds within words and to manipulate them. There are about 44 phonemes (different sounds) in the English language. Phonic approaches to learning reading have been popular in the past. It is now generally accepted that phonic awareness is an important component of reading development, but that it should be combined with reading experience, using the other 'searchlights' described above.

Learning sounds (phonological awareness) is part of the development of phonics. Phonics is the knowledge of the link between sounds (phonemes) and letters (graphemes), the development of which is a crucial step in decoding text. Children develop phonic awareness both in infancy and in pre-school settings, through rhymes, stories, poems and songs. For example, pre-school children develop this awareness through learning and making up rhymes, and through alliteration e.g. such as 'the dinosaur Donald drew a donut on the dresser'. Success or problems in these early stages are important predictors of how a child's reading development will progress. Phonological awareness helps children to link the sounds in spoken words to the written words they are learning to read.

In order to develop phonological awareness, children need to learn the alphabet and to learn phonemes, which are the separate sounds in words. They also need to learn about syllables and onset and rime. Rohl (2000: 69 Table 3.2) demonstrates the different levels of phonological awareness as follows:

Syllable	cat-er-pil-lar
Onset-rime	c-at, sl-ip
Phoneme	c-a-t, s-l-i-p

Onset is the first sound in a syllable and rime is the vowel and all that follows it. For example, b (onset) and ag (rime) or st (onset) and ag (rime). Onset can be used to produce alliteration ('Stringy Stan stopped a stallion stealing stubble'). Rimes are the bit of the syllable which can be used to make rhymes (bag, stag, nag, lag, crag).

Beard (1993: 94) argues that the development of the ability to distinguish between onset and rime, which often takes place pre-school, is a crucial precursor to learning to read and write. However, children seem to learn the smallest units, phonemes, through the actual process of learning to read and write. As such, some levels of phonological awareness are already developed to some extent in many children before they start school, such as being able to clap out syllables and distinguish onset and rime. Children who have difficulties with these early stages may need extra help with learning to read and write and may have problems with recognizing sounds. Rohl (2000: 69) supports this view: 'Various research studies have shown that the ability to recognise the units of onset and rime at the pre-school stage is related to children's success in later reading and spelling (Goswami and Bryant, 1990).'

Learning sounds correctly is an important part of developing phonological awareness. For example, Terry, at age 6, was still struggling to hear sounds effectively. Although he was a highly verbal child, an early ear problem had left his hearing depressed. Terry often misheard first sounds of new words. He could not always repeat new words correctly or be able to hear the boundaries between words in speech. For a long time he believed that 'cupoftea' was all one word. He also had persistent problems with identifying the last sounds in words. These difficulties had a marked effect on both his confidence and ability to tackle reading.

Many children have early pronunciation difficulties with certain words, some of which can continue for years. The author's 9-year-old still pronounces 'bracelet' as 'raceplut' despite increasingly exasperated efforts to correct herself. However, most children eventually learn correct pronunciation and the ability to distinguish between words in a sentence, and the mistakes they make earlier on diminish. Learning the link between the spoken and written word depends on good pronunciation and the ability to hear separate sounds in words.

6.1 Learning the alphabet

Children who know the alphabet before they start school are likely to do well in reading and writing. Learning the alphabet at home or in pre-school is often supported by:

- Alphabet songs.

- Visual displays of the alphabet.

- Individual letters linked to pictures which act as clues e.g. posters showing the alphabet and pictures of objects beginning with each letter.

- Alphabet jigsaws.

- Alphabet games e.g. matching letter and picture cards; groups of children sort themselves into alphabetical order either by carrying large letters or using their names.

- Use of a multi-sensory approach e.g. modelling, painting, drawing in sand, tracing letters.

These activities can continue in school and are particularly useful for children who have a shaky grasp of the alphabet.

6.2 Supporting the development of phonological awareness

The *National Literacy Strategy: Progression in Phonics* (DfEE, 2000a: 7) guidelines state that phonics should be the key focus of the fifteen-minute word-level part of the literacy hour. Phonics instruction needs to be done 'away from texts', through play, games and activities, and then applied to shared and guided reading along with the other 'searchlights'.

The role of classroom assistants is suggested by the guidelines. They can:

1. Join in and keep the pace up.

2. Model responses.

3. Run the activity with the teacher.

4. Ask searching questions if some children have not understood.

5. Check which children are secure in their knowledge and which are not.

6. Support individual children.

7. Take notes or observe.

8. Work with small groups needing extra help.

The sorts of activities that promote the development of phonological awareness are:

- Using, making up and repeating sounds.

- Any activity which uses rhyme e.g. finding rhymes for words or rhyming phrases (Jammy Pammy, Strong Pong).

- Any activity which uses alliteration e.g. adding words on to sentences like 'Wally went walking on Wednesday ... .'

- Activities which involve matching phonemes e.g. to objects with the same first sound – a range of objects are given out and the children hold up their object if the first sound matches the adult's object.

- Activities which involve matching sounds to letters e.g. adult or child writing letters to match sounds in words.

- 'I spy with my little eye' to establish knowledge and practise recognition of first sounds.

A chance to think

Activities aimed at developing phonological awareness are often based on encouraging children to listen to initial sounds (phonemes) and then match them to other words with the same sounds. The children can then be encouraged to recognize other sounds in words, and then to link the sounds to written letters through different types of activities.

Exercise 3.5

During the literacy hour observe the children during activities aimed at raising phonological awareness. Which children are confident in their knowledge? Which children need extra help? Consider activities that may best support the children who need extra help and discuss your ideas with the teacher or a mentor. Refer to the *National Literacy Strategy: Progression in Phonics* (DfEE, 2000a) guidelines for ideas to extend or adapt.

The National Curriculum for English Key Stage 1 states that children need to 'hear, identify, segment and blend phonemes in words'. 'Segmenting' refers to the ability to break words down into their component sounds. For example, p-a-r-a-ch-u-te. 'Blending' refers to the ability to put the sounds together and pronounce the word. It is sometimes referred to as 'sounding out' and is an important skill for tackling new words in unfamiliar text where the other 'searchlights' are not strong.

Children can be supported in this process by:

- Encouragement to tackle new words.
- Praise for success.
- Prompts for when the child gets stuck e.g. asking the child to remember what the phoneme sounds like.
- Reminders of different contexts in which the word might be found.
- Reminding the child to sound out, not spell out, the word in order to be able to blend the sounds for meaning.
- Checking the child has used all other available clues to the meaning of the word.

6.3 Grammatical knowledge

One of the clues which children bring to bear on text, in order to find meaning or cross-check their guesses at meaning, is their knowledge of grammar and how text works. Children learn the rules of sentence structure from spoken language and being read to. As such, they become aware of the ways in which sentences are likely to be constructed. This knowledge is a crucial tool for deciphering the meaning of text.

For example, a child may recognize that in the sentence 'I went to the shop' it is likely that a verb will follow 'I'. Although the child may not have a clue what a verb is, he/she knows the type of words that are likely to be next in the sequence. Miscues (mistakes) in reading this sentence may include saying other words with the same initial sound such as 'wanted', which also contain some of the same letters. However, it is likely that if the child does misread the word, he/she will substitute another verb for 'went', because his/her grammatical knowledge will tell him/her that this is the type of word that comes next.

Grammatical knowledge develops as children read more and become familiar with a range of texts. Clearly, grammatical knowledge is a rough guide to the meaning of words within text, but taken along with the other tools the child is developing, it can help to support children's guesses.

6.4 Knowledge of context

Other clues which children use are their knowledge of the context in which the word is embedded. This means that children will cross-check their other clues to meaning by using a word that is likely to be next in the text, in line with the story line or discussion taking place. Pictures are important clues to context in the earlier stages of reading. For example, a child may read the familiar word 'The' easily in a sentence starting 'The children swam' and then seek further clues to the unfamiliar word 'children'. She/he may draw on what she/he knows about grammar, any pictures and the context of the sentence, and a tentative 'sounding out' of the phoneme 'ch'. This will probably give a fairly confident child enough to go on and she/he will try out 'children'.

6.5 Word recognition and graphic knowledge

Children learn many words as whole units rather than as a blend of phonemes, usually early on in their reading experience. Some words are learned in the environment prior to the child entering school as described above. Although learning words in this way does not support the development of phonological awareness to any great extent, the process of recognizing some words by sight can help children to make a start with reading.

Children often learn key words from the school's chosen reading scheme as a way of building confidence in tackling text. Flash cards are used for the child to memorize the shape and appearance of the groups of letters. Because this process does not demand an understanding of sounds, children can learn words by sight before they have a confident grasp of the alphabet. Critics of the process argue that children can be bored by endless flash cards and overloaded by repetitive rote learning. Words that are to be learned by sight are listed for each year of Key Stage 1 in the *National Literacy Strategy: Framework for Teaching*, under 'word recognition' (DfEE, 1998).

It is important that word recognition is not overly relied on or that it becomes boring for the children. It is a useful tool for helping children to start reading and build confidence in understanding the content of text, but ultimately children need to gain phonological awareness in order to tackle unfamiliar words successfully.

Children may start to recognize letters from their sounds as part of their learning of sight words. This is to be encouraged as children start to apply their phonic knowledge to words they know.

6.6 Supporting the development of word recognition

Children can be supported in the development of word recognition through:

- Matching whole sentences to those in books.

- Cutting up and muddling words in a sentence and then reorganizing them into sentences to match sentences in books.

- Comparing words on flash cards to see if they are the same.

- Muddling up words from a sentence and asking children to put them back in order.

- Making up and reading silly sentences.

- Using appropriate computer software.

7. READING WITH CHILDREN

However diverse the role of the teaching assistant, it is very likely that you will spend a lot of time reading with children. This is a crucial part of the development of reading skills for individual children, but it can also be important in identifying children with reading problems and delays. The value of listening to children read is high:

- The child enjoys individual attention.

- You can check progress and levels of ability.

- You can observe the strategies the child uses to tackle text and where they may need help to develop these further.

- You can give praise and encourage the child.

- You can talk about the story to ensure the child is reading for meaning and enjoying the book.

- The child can gain confidence from your feedback.

- Reluctant readers can be identified.

- Children with significant reading problems can be identified.

- You can report back important information about the child's reading ability to the teacher.

It is likely that you will be involved in reading with individual and groups of children. However, whatever reading activities you do with children it is important to keep a record, within the school system for recording reading progress, which reflects progress and concerns. It is also important to keep a record of the books a child has read so that he/she is progressing at a steady pace and not stuck on one book he/she knows well or leaping ahead of his/her ability. Some children benefit from using suitable software to develop their word recognition or phonic awareness, and teaching assistants may be involved in supporting children in this way. It is important to take time to familiarize yourself with the benefits and limitations of different software packages, and to consider what they can contribute to children's literacy development. It is also important to use the right package to meet the specific needs of individual children.

7.1   Differentiation

One of the challenging tasks that face many teaching assistants is to differentiate the class activities to meet the needs of particular groups of children. Differentiation is the process by which tasks are extended or made simpler to meet a range of needs in the classroom, rather than expecting all children to be at the same stage of development. Often teaching assistants work with children who need more support with the elements of the task. Differentiation is sometimes achieved by some children getting teaching assistant support and others not. However, tasks can be differentiated by:

- Additional elements of the task are introduced to extend some children e.g. children are asked to draw a number of different types of houses after looking at pictures, reading and talking as a whole group. It is suggested that some children write captions to their pictures.

- More or less specific instructions depending on the ability of the children to work independently.

- Working alongside individual children or groups to make suggestions, keep up pace and praise interim progress.

A *chance to think*

Differentiation can be crucial to ensuring that children progress at their own pace, and are not left floundering during class activities. Children who feel they cannot tackle the class tasks may lose self-confidence and develop low self-esteem in relation to their learning ability. In the long term this could lead to non-compliance and even school refusal. It is important that children who need extra help are given this in a tactful and sympathetic way which supports their learning but does not leave them feeling stigmatized.

Exercise 3.6

In a Year 1 class there are about six children who are making slower progress with reading and writing than the rest of the class. For some parts of the day they sit together on Yellow table. Today, the class have been talking about themselves and their personal characteristics. The children have been asked to draw themselves and write something about themselves and then to repeat this activity by drawing a partner and writing something about them. They are then going to discuss their work as a whole group and look at differences between children. You are working with the group of children who are sitting on Yellow table.

1. Describe how you could help the children feel comfortable with extra help.

2. What sort of help would you offer them?

3. How might you adapt the task to suit their needs?

4. How would you help the children progress and gain from the task?

Discuss your ideas with a colleague or mentor and check the sample answers on page 165.

8. WRITING

The development of writing skills is closely linked to the process of learning to read. Current thinking about the ways in which writing is learned and taught acknowledge that the development of handwriting, spelling and punctuation need to go hand in hand with the development of understanding about the various purposes of writing and different forms of writing. Bentley *et al.* (1999: 102) describe these two aspects of writing as:

- The composing/creative aspects of writing.
- The performing/secretarial aspects of writing.

The first refers to the content and purpose of writing, how the piece is written and the creative elements within it. For example, the quality of the composition of a story in terms of imagination, plot, characterization and balance between beginning, middle and end. The second refers to the technical skills required to write legibly, such as handwriting, spelling and punctuation. Beard (1993: 182) reminds us that the 'secretarial' aspect should not be seen as more important than the 'authorial' aspect. There must be a balance between the two. Support materials for developing writing as part of the National Literacy Strategy include *Developing Early Writing* which, like *Progression in Phonics*, includes a CD-ROM (DfEE, 2001). In these guidelines, two phases of writing are described:

- Composition – planning what to write, who the writing is for and the purpose of the writing.
- Transcription – spelling, handwriting.

These are closely linked to the teaching and learning skills described above.

8.1 Developing Writing

Children start the process of writing early on through their play and through imitation of adults and other children. This may take the form of purposeful mark-making, where children make marks that they perceive to have meaning. Children are demonstrating their understanding of the purposes of writing by making these marks in contexts where writing is relevant. This could be list-making, message writing or note-taking either in role play or real life situations. In this way, children are demonstrating that they understand what writing is for. By 'reading' what they have 'written' children also demonstrate that they know that writing symbolizes spoken language. Children learn symbolic behaviour through play in their early years, developing the ability to recognize that one thing can represent another thing. For example, when a child takes up a stick and says, 'This is my sword/gun/wand' on different occasions, he/she is showing his/her understanding of the ways in which the stick can symbolize other things. Activities such as these are important in developing understanding of symbolic representation.

Play is an important medium for developing writing in pre-school and at Key Stage 1. Children can be encouraged to use writing in play situations as a way of building confidence and recognizing the uses of writing. For example, labelling and message taking in role play.

Developing writing can be supported by adults through:

- Modelling writing by using writing for a range of purposes with children.

- Using writing across the widest range of activities.

- Discussing the purposes of writing and demonstrating these.

- Providing ideas and experiences and other reasons for children to write.

- Filling the environment with print.

- Reading across a range of texts.

- Using appropriate computer software.

8.2 Stages of writing development

1. Children recognize the purposes of writing and that writing is speech recorded as print. They are mark-making as a purposeful activity and starting to write their own names.

2. Children are using letters in their mark-making to represent sounds and are writing some short familiar words.

3. Children are writing more words and starting to use their writing to communicate in different ways, although this can be repetitious.

4. Writing is becoming more fluent and being used for a range of purposes.

For example, at the age of five, Amy wrote her name and could write letters of the alphabet. At six she was writing more words and creating sentences to explain or describe different things or as a story. Her weekly diary work showed the same words repeatedly used in short sentences to describe her home activities e.g. 'I went to the gym with my mum'. By seven, Amy had developed a wider range of words and was tackling new words confidently, checking her spelling with a first dictionary and writing for a wider range of purposes. She was also using writing in a range of computer games and educational packages.

8.3 Shared writing

Shared writing is an important method of teaching writing skills. Children can be involved in planning stories, drafting and revising what is written. The children contribute to the story and the teacher writes it down, discussing choices of words and sentences and developing the flow of the story. Shared writing makes an important contribution to the children's understanding of composition, but it also gives children a chance to experience the transition from spoken word to written word. Children sometimes write during shared writing, often on individual wipeable whiteboards. Shared writing can also help children with spelling and can strengthen their phonological awareness.

8.4 Supporting writing development

The teaching assistant's role will inevitably involve a substantial amount of support for children's writing development. This should be in the context of the school's policy on how children should write and form letters and the ways this will be taught. There are a number of important issues that need to be considered in helping children with writing:

- Does the child know what he/she is writing about?
- Does the child know who he/she is writing for?
- Does the child know or can he/she see key words?
- Has the type of writing to be used been modelled?
- Has there been enough discussion about the content and approach to the writing, the topic and structure and how the writing may be sequenced?

Children need to have opportunities to read from a range of texts to start to recognize different types of writing. These could include poetry, non-fiction, instruction manuals and stories. In this way, children start to develop a sense of how to approach their own writing for different purposes. It is important to:

- Discuss with children the different uses of writing and how these can be identified.
- Discuss with children how they are going to approach the writing task.
- Plan the content, however brief.
- Discuss drafts and redrafts.

The teaching assistant's role in supporting writing can include:

1. Scribing for children – this means writing for children who are composing, giving the child freedom from the transcription task in order to develop composition skills. Bentley *et al.* (1999: 107) suggest that when children are asked to copy the adult's writing it will restrict their desire to compose at length as they know they will have to copy a lot of words. Scribing for children means they can compose at length and develop composition skills without the distraction of writing.

2. Supporting guided writing with individual children or groups – working with

children needing additional support or children who can extend their ideas and compose and write more independently.

3. Supporting independent writing – working with children who may not be ready to tackle independent writing, by scribing for them, encouraging planning through discussion and helping children to gain confidence to tackle independent writing though praise and positive feedback.

4. Helping children to access computer software designed to support writing development.

5. Supporting the development of spelling.

8.5 Supporting the development of spelling

Children learn to spell as part of the more general process of learning to read and write, and as part of specific strategies to develop spelling. It is important that the drive towards correct spelling does not inhibit children in their developing writing. In the example above, Amy stuck to her diary entry because it was tried and tested. She could spell all the words and the sentence produced met the requirements of the task. However, she needed to progress further and take risks in her writing. In order to do this, Amy had to be convinced that it was acceptable to make mistakes sometimes.

Teaching assistants working with individual or groups of children can support spelling by:

- Praising successful efforts.

- Praising good 'tries'.

- Working with children on 'Look, Say, Cover, Think, Write and Check'.

- Diagnosing spelling mistakes and talking to children about how these occur.

- Checking work with children and talking about words they are unsure of.

- Correcting errors.

- Helping children to use computer packages that support spelling development.

However, it is important to consider how much direct correction is helpful to a child. Focusing on a limited number of spelling errors and encouraging the child to identify these for herself is a better approach than meticulously correcting every mistake.

8.6 Supporting the development of handwriting

As discussed above, children are usually mark-making and sometimes shaping letters before they start school. Many children become interested in putting pencil to paper through experiences at home or pre-school. These early efforts should be praised and encouraged, as they are an important part of the development of handwriting. Supporting handwriting development includes:

- Ensuring children are comfortably seated and have their paper at an appropriate angle (this will be different for left- and right-handed children).

- Ensuring the child holds the pencil correctly and that the child has the right size of pencil for easy grip (children who have problems with this may benefit from fitting a pencil grip to a standard pencil or writing with a thicker pencil).

- Helping children to practise shaping letters (finding the starting point, moving the pencil in the correct sequence of directions).

- Correcting repeated mistakes in letter formation (these can become embedded).

- Modelling letter formation and talking about this with the child.

- Praising and encouraging handwriting.

For some children, the physical process of writing may inhibit the development of writing overall. The child may know what he wants to write and even be able to 'see' the words, but for a range of reasons, find it difficult to actually shape the letters by hand. This may be because of a specific physical disability or because the child has specific learning disabilities. The child may be dyspraxic (clumsy) or dyslexic (have difficulty translating mental images of letters onto paper), or there may be other special educational needs that inhibit the development of the scribing process. For these children, carefully chosen computer software may be of great help. The child may be able to progress with the other aspects of writing and develop creativity, without the limitations of not being able to handwrite effectively. Clearly, this type of support needs to be linked to continuing development of handwriting, but it can be very helpful in supporting confidence and good self-esteem in children who cannot write.

9. THE TEACHING ASSISTANT'S ROLE IN THE LITERACY HOUR

Teaching assistants sometimes have a specific role in supporting children and the teacher during the various stages of the literacy hour (as discussed in Chapter 1). This may be because the children are young, or the class is large, or there are a number of children with SEN or who are multi-lingual in the class. Teaching assistants may support the progress of the literacy hour in a number of ways, which include:

During whole class teaching:

- Joining in and encouraging the children to join in.

- Encouraging shy children to make contributions.

- Repeating instructions when children are unclear.

- Sitting with and supporting individual children.

- Ensuring all the children are paying attention and gently curbing whispering and fiddling.

- Managing resources in line with the teacher's requirements, for example, distributing books, props or pencils.

During small group and individual work:

- Repeating instructions and breaking them down into small stages.
- Helping children start the task.
- Encouraging children to concentrate and keep up pace.
- Answering questions.
- Giving praise.
- Discouraging distracting behaviour.

The teaching assistant may be involved in planning the session with the teacher, and should also give feedback on the pupil's progress and the effectiveness of the session, any problems that arose, and where the need for further differentiation has arisen. Teaching assistants are frequently asked to support children in the class who have learning delays or special educational needs, or who lack the skills or confidence to tackle new tasks. Often children are in need of reminders, prompts, positive feedback on their progress and the support of an interested adult in order to tackle new tasks. There are some good examples of supporting children in the literacy hour in Section 6 of *The Teaching Assistant's File* (DfEE, 2000b).

CONCLUSIONS

Supporting the development of literacy skills is one of the key tasks of a teaching assistant. Using a range of interpersonal skills and a sound knowledge of the processes by which children become literate, you can be invaluable in helping children to make confident progress with this sometimes challenging area of learning. Helping children discover the pleasures of reading books, poems, non-fiction and information about the world around them can give them a lifelong personal and career resource. Helping children to compose their own written work and to develop their imaginative and creative skills can be of great benefit to their self-esteem and confidence.

In busy classes, both children and teachers can benefit from the contributions of a teaching assistant, and you are ideally placed to give feedback to the teacher on any problems or difficulties children are experiencing.

NOTES FOR FURTHER READING

Barratt-Pugh, C. (2000a)
'The socio-cultural context of literacy learning', Chapter 1 in Barratt-Pugh, C. and Rohl, M. (eds) *Literacy Learning In the Early Years*.
Milton Keynes: Open University Press.

Barratt-Pugh, C. (2000b)
'Literacies in more than one language', Chapter 8 in Barratt-Pugh, C. and Rohl, M. (eds) *Literacy Learning In the Early Years*.
Milton Keynes: Open University Press.

Beard, R. (1993)
Teaching Literacy, Balancing Perspectives.
London: Hodder and Stoughton.

Bentley, D., Chamberlin, R., Gray, D., Lynch, M., Burmam, C., Clipson-Boyles, S., Holderness, J. and Reid, D. (1999)
The Really Practical Guide to English.
Cheltenham: Nelson Thornes.

Bielby, N. (1998)
How to Teach Reading – a Balanced Approach.
Leamington Spa: Scholastic Ltd.

DfEE (1998)
National Literacy Strategy: Framework for Teaching.
Nottingham: DfEE

DfEE (1999)
National Literacy Strategy: Talking in Class, NLS Flier 1.
Nottingham: DfEE.

DfEE (2000a)
National Literacy Strategy: Progression in Phonics.
Nottingham: DfEE.

DfEE, (2000b)
The Teaching Assistant's File.
Nottingham: DfEE.

DfEE (2001)
National Literacy Strategy: Developing Early Writing.
Nottingham: DfEE.

Goswamy U. and Bryant, P. (1990)
Phono Logical Skills and Learning to Read.
Hove: Lawrence Erlbaum.

McNaughton, S. (1995)
Patterns of Emergent Literacy.
Melbourne: Oxford University Press.

O'Hara, M. (2000)
Teaching 3–8.
London: Continuum.

Qualifications and Curriculum Authority (QCA) (2000)
Curriculum Guidance for the Foundation Stage.
Sudbury: QCA.

Rohl, M. (2000)
Learning About Words, Sounds and Letters, Chapter 3 in Barratt-Pugh, C. and Rohl, M. (eds) *Literacy Learning In the Early Years.*
Milton Keynes: Open University Press.

Vygotsky, L. (1978)
Mind and Society.
Cambridge, MA: Harvard University Press.

CHAPTER 4

Supporting Key Stage 1 Maths

INTRODUCTION

Maths is one of the core skills children start to develop early in life. Activities in the child's home such as counting games and rhymes, sorting and matching activities and 'sharing out' all give young children an opportunity to start to understand number names and their meanings. These activities are extended and built on in pre-school settings, where children are encouraged to learn about shape, measure, sorting of objects and relationships between objects as part of the Foundation Stage curriculum for 3- to 5-year-olds. However, studies show that children need support and encouragement to focus on number – they do not do this naturally. Therefore, there is a very particular need for appropriate intervention to ensure that children learn mathematical principles during their early years (Munn and Schaffer, 1993).

Maths is often perceived as something we do with paper and a pen, but early mathematical concepts can be learned before the child has the ability to represent maths problems symbolically. Children can learn a great deal about number through practical work and the development of mental number work before they have mastered the skill of writing numbers down in a meaningful way. Mental maths and understanding of mathematical concepts are crucial to underpinnings to progress in this area.

The teaching and learning of maths is not always straightforward. The Cockcroft Report (DES, 1982) found that many people found themselves unable to master the practical applications of maths in 'real life' situations. Part of the problem may be adults' own feelings about maths and misconceptions about mathematical concepts. Adults involved in teaching, and supporting the teaching, of maths may not necessarily feel confident to do so, or may feel that the teaching and learning of maths is something of an ordeal (Haylock and Cockburn, 1997). There are many ways of teaching and learning mathematical skills and concepts, and teaching is found to be most effective when a range of methods is used (Griffiths, 1994).

Anyone who has had a child in school will probably have been told at some stage that 'we don't do it that way at school' when you try and help your child with maths problems at home. Different terms for the processes involved in solving maths problems can also confuse children. Think of all the terms for subtraction – take away, less than, fewer than and so on. Children can often struggle with their understanding of mathematical concepts unless the foundations have been learned well.

The Numeracy Strategy and the numeracy hour were introduced in schools in 1999 as a method of trying to raise standards in terms of the teaching and learning of mathematics. The numeracy hour is not the only time that maths is learned in school. Maths problems should be introduced across the curriculum and integrated into a range of other subject areas. However, there is now a clear emphasis on whole class teaching within the numeracy hour as the main method of teaching mathematics.

1. LEARNING MATHS AT HOME

Babies and toddlers can learn a great deal about maths in the home through everyday activities which reinforce their understanding of counting and quantity, measurement and time. Some parents will use numbers in their day-to-day inter-actions with children, counting objects, people, the stairs on the way to bed, the biscuits left in the tin. Children learn that quantities can increase and decrease and that there is a relationship between counting words (one, two, three ...) and actual quantity. For example, Ginny, at the age of three, went for a hearing test. For every sound she heard through the headphones she was asked to put a wooden figure in a boat. She performed the task with great accuracy, having considerable experience of matching sounds to objects by this age. Young children learn about distance and about the size and shape of objects around them through everyday activities with parents. Words like 'big' and 'small' start to gain their relative meanings, and very many young children learn the concept of 'just one more' early on in their development, often in connection with something nice to eat!

Everyday life teaches children about relative measurements of distance ('It's a long way to Nan's house, but a short way to Aunty Jo's'), about shape ('The roundabout is round and it goes around') and about the pattern of the day ('Playgroup is in the morning, nap is after lunch'). Pound (1999) suggests that when babies are starting to walk they learn a great deal about space and distance as they move between objects and towards objects. Children learn about time through experience ('just five more minutes in the playground') and through their growing recognition of the role of clocks and watches in 'telling the time'.

Children also become familiar with a broad range of environmental numerals, becoming increasingly aware of the link between these symbols and numbers. For example, numbers on buses, digital clocks, numbers on phones and car number plates. Songs, nursery rhymes and stories support the child's growing understanding of the relationships of numbers, counting one to ten, and counting numbers of objects. Children very much enjoy counting objects on pages and naming the number, and through repetition of this process they start to learn accurate counting skills as described below. By the time they are about three, the majority of children will have the basis of a practical working knowledge of many mathematical concepts, which they can apply in everyday situations.

However, the extent to which children gain this early basis for mathematical learning depends on the quality of their early experiences and the parenting they receive. Children who have limited experience, or who have difficulties or dis-advantages in their early lives, may miss out on this crucial grounding in mathematical concepts. It is important to remember that some children may enter pre-school or even school without having the benefit of these early experiences, and this may disadvantage them significantly. Perhaps one of the most important ways in which children learn about basis maths is through conversation with parents and others about the day-to-day applications of number, shape, time and space. Children from families with poor patterns of communication may be among the most disadvantaged in this area.

2. MATHS IN THE FOUNDATION STAGE FOR 3- TO 5-YEAR-OLDS

Mathematical development is one of the areas of learning within the curriculum for the Foundation Stage. The *Curriculum Guidance for the Foundation Stage* (QCA, 2000) emphasizes that children should learn about maths across the curriculum and not just through activities specifically designed to develop mathematical skills and thinking. Areas for mathematical development include:

- The use of numbers as 'labels' and accurate counting.

- Calculating – manipulating numbers in practical activities to start to recognize the processes of addition, subtraction, division and multiplication.

- Shape, space, measure and time.

The National Numeracy Strategy Key Objectives for reception classes are the same as the Early Learning Goals (ELG) for maths, within the Foundation Stage, providing a common curriculum for reception classes between the two stages. In the Foundation Stage there is an emphasis on learning mathematical ideas through play and practical activities. Recording is considered to be less important and does not have to be the recording of numerals. Children may draw pictures of objects or use non-numerical symbols. Hughes (1986) discusses the ways in which young children learn to create symbols to represent numbers. These can be tally-marks or pictures or other marks that are meaningful for the child. At this stage, there is no pressure on children to use numerals to record.

Practical activities can focus on singing and counting rhymes that support children's understanding of the relationship between numbers and a quantity of objects. Visual representations that emphasize the link between numerals and the number of objects, for example, posters, pictures and borders that show 1 apple, 2 birds, 3 rabbits and so on, are also useful in reinforcing children's learning in this area.

Matching activities can help children to develop an understanding of the properties of different shapes. Focusing on environmental shapes can be an important part of shape recognition. One 4-year-old became very adept at finding shapes in the environment after a session at nursery. She could see triangles and other shapes in buildings and in the shadows between buildings, and identified the shape of every car window, shop front and a myriad of other environmental features. This process reinforced her knowledge and understanding and helped her relate her nursery learning to her real life. Children also benefit a great deal from mathematical types of conversations at this stage, as they do at home. This includes conversations about shape, size and relative size, time and space, length, depth and width, numbers and counting, shares and adding and subtracting. These conversations can be part of specific activities designed to develop mathematical thinking, but should also be part of the regular day-to-day interactions that take place between educarers and the children.

The extent to which children develop mathematical thinking in their pre-school years is linked to their cultural context and the range and type of experiences they have as infants. Pound (1999: 6) comments that young children's growing ability with mathematical thinking 'depends heavily on the experiences, social interactions and accompanying language that children meet in these formative years'

Linking home and pre-school experience and building on children's own interests are crucially important to help children develop mathematical thinking. For example, at age 3, Jason first noticed that the level of the bath water went down when he got out. He then went on to notice, unprompted, that the level went up and down to different extents, when different members of the family got in and out of the bath. He puzzled as to why this was and came to the conclusion that it was the size of the person that affected the change of level. He also concluded that it was not just the height of the person that dictated the level, but also their width. Jason went on to discover when bathing with his sister that the level went down when he got out and further down when she got out. By this time, Jason had done considerable work on understanding volume. When he mentioned this at nursery school, the teacher did an activity in which the children were involved in displacing different amounts of water with different objects, which supported, extended and consolidated Jason's own learning. Jason talked about his observations and what conclusions he had drawn from them, and was very proud when the rest of his group came back with bath-time water level stories the next day.

The possibility of delays in developing mathematical thinking due to poor quality early experiences is discussed above. However, it is important to remember that children may develop different understanding of maths or have different experiences of developing mathematical thinking, depending on their social and cultural environment at home. It is not helpful, therefore, to make any assumptions about what children know, how they know it and how they can express their knowledge, as this may differ a great deal between children for a whole range of complex and interlinked reasons.

Many of the types of practical activities children have experienced in the Foundation Stage can be developed at Key Stage 1 to give the children continuity in their learning.

2.1 Learning maths through play

In the early years, play is a key learning method for the development of mathematical thinking. Edwards (1998: 1) states that:

> For young children, learning is about developing a sense of meaning and understanding of the world around them. It represents, predominantly, a social process where the highest incidence of learning takes place in social settings, in the company of interested adults and other children. (Bruner, 1990)

Play provides children with the social context for learning, in which they can develop skills, knowledge and understanding. Using play as a context for mathematical learning gives children the opportunity to develop their curiosity, share ideas and knowledge, and have their misconceptions corrected. Play, therefore, gives children the opportunity to develop their practical knowledge of maths in a structured, social environment. At Key Stage 1, where practical and mental maths are developed before written maths (see below), play is a useful starting point to develop the concrete basis on which children build their later, more abstract mathematical understanding.

Children not only constantly use mathematical skills within play, such as counting, sharing, measuring and comparing, but they also practise their understanding of the social uses of numbers in context, such as 'making phone calls' or 'paying at the shops'. Griffiths (1994) identified five advantages of learning maths through play in the early years:

- Play is purposeful and learning maths through play will have purpose.

- Maths is based on abstract concepts and play can help the child link the abstract and the concrete.

- Children take control in play, problem-solving and organizing themselves, which are valuable tools for learning maths.

- Play gives children opportunity to master and assimilate mathematical concepts.

- Practical activities, rather than written records, are the medium for children to develop mathematical knowledge and understanding.

The use of number can be included in a wide range of planned and free play, and children will spontaneously use the mathematical concepts they know in their imaginative play, as it arises in context. Warren and Westmoreland (2000) suggest that role play is a medium through which children will demonstrate and practise their maths knowledge and skills because they use meaningful contexts within this type of play.

For example, Declan and Danny, five, are playing at trains. With help from Aisha, seven, they arrange a ticket booth and tickets and start to charge customers to travel on the trains. They charge five pence per ticket per customer, using coins. They issue one ticket per person on receipt of the five pence. They also accept combinations of different coins to make up the five pence cost of the ticket. During the play their learning is reinforced in these areas:

- One-to-one correlation – five pence per ticket per customer.

- That five pence is sometimes symbolized by the 5p coin.

- That different coins add up to five pence.

- That larger size coins do not necessarily have greater value than smaller ones.

Children may also show their understanding of mathematical concepts during play when this is not so evident at other times. For example, during a game in which a group of children were setting up a pavement stall to 'sell' a range of items, the youngest, aged 4, got involved in labelling the items with prices. She had an older 'scribe' to write the prices on the sticky labels, but it was the 4-year-old who was making judgements about the relative value of different items and the prices that should go with the different values. Her parents did not know that she had this level of understanding until they observed the game. Young children can also learn through simple board games, such as those that include the use of dice and space counting as part of the game. For example, playing the board game 'Snakes and

Ladders' involves developing the following maths skills:

- Counting the number of dots on the face of the dice after it is thrown.
- Increasingly developing sight recognition of the number value of the cluster of dots on each face of the dice.
- Acquiring the skills to accurately count the number of places according to the number on the dice, ensuring one space count matches one number name.

It is important when playing board games with young children to concentrate on the process, not the outcome, and to ensure that the children have time to work out their counting and to count the dots on the dice. Telling them the answers or moving dice for them will not support any real learning (Griffiths, 1994: 153). Edwards (1998) suggests that it is important that children have the opportunity to both learn new knowledge about maths through either structured activities or free play, and also to master and practise new ideas by applying them in different contexts, in order to give depth to their understanding. Balancing both these types of play is important to ensure children learn new things about maths, but can also apply what they know in 'real life' situations. For example, the class could work on addition to ten by adding together different combinations of ten small objects. This practical activity can help children to start to recognize number bonds to ten. The children could then play at 'shops', giving change from ten pence for a range of differently priced items.

Perhaps one of the major challenges that children and those responsible for their learning face is the transition from this practically based mode of learning, rooted in everyday experience, to the more abstract and conceptual approach to maths that they experience at later stages.

3. KEY STAGE 1 MATHEMATICS

Guidance as to teaching and learning mathematics at Key Stage 1 can be found in the *National Curriculum for England and Wales* (DfEE/QCA, 1999) and the *National Numeracy Strategy: Framework for Teaching Mathematics* (DfEE, 1999a) which describes what should be taught in each year, and how it should be taught. The Numeracy Strategy is based on four key principles:

- Dedicated mathematics lessons every day.
- Direct teaching and interactive oral work with the whole class and groups.
- An emphasis on mental calculation.
- Controlled differentiation, with all pupils engaged in mathematics relating to a common theme.

At Key Stage 1, there are two attainment targets for mathematics. These are:

- number
- shape, space and measures.

3.1 Approaches to maths

Children learn about maths through practical experiences, play and everyday activities in their early years. This early learning is supported by children's talk about maths, as they learn the language of maths and develop mental strategies to deal with numbers in different ways. Pound (1999) argues that it is important that the transition to school maths should include building on children's previous experiences to move from the concrete to the abstract, as a number of studies show that children can lose their enthusiasm for maths at this stage. This may be due to a dislocation between the things children know about maths in their environment and what they actually do at school. Edwards (1998: 9) states that, in relation to teaching and learning maths: 'Children should be encouraged to articulate their ideas, ask questions, listen to and follow instructions; and to share challenges in discussion with their friends and teachers at every stage.'

In order to maintain this important approach to learning about maths, the emphasis on written maths problems (such as sums) has become less important at Key Stage 1 than mental and oral work. This approach allows children to develop mathematical skills without keeping them to rigid stages of representation. Children can record their maths work using pictures, icons or symbols, allowing them to develop mathematical understanding without being constrained by the limitations on their ability to record at the 'appropriate stage'. Children choose their own form of representation to answer a wide variety of problems. Put simply, the child's ability to answer maths problems can outstrip his/her ability to record the answers; therefore, children should be able to answer maths problems without having to be able to write them down in a conventional way. It is important not to confuse 'formal number operations and recording' with the ability to understand number (O'Hara, 2000).

Haylock and Cockburn (1997) developed a model to try and clarify the different types of experiences of maths which children may have. These are:

- concrete experiences

- language

- symbols

- pictures.

For example, children may learn addition by having a number of objects, say marbles, which they can count and add onto. By using the marbles, they have concrete experience of adding, for example, four marbles and two marbles to make six. In addition, the children could draw a picture of the groups of four marbles and two marbles and these added together to make six marbles. The children could write the addition down as a sum, using symbols so that they write $4 + 2 = 6$. Finally, the children can talk about the processes, using the language of maths, describing and clarifying what they are doing and sharing ideas with each other. It is the combination of these different types of experiences that helps children learn about mathematical concepts. Therefore, the use of a range of different approaches to teaching and learning maths is very important, because it extends the different types of experiences children have and this builds up and reinforces their understanding of mathematical concepts.

Edwards (1998) suggests a similar model for making the connections between the concrete, practically based mathematical understanding children begin with, and the more abstract and conceptual understanding of maths that they need to progress to. There is some evidence that children may lose their confidence and become less able at maths if this transition in approach and understanding is not effective. Language seems to be a key element in this transition, not only by children learning mathematical language, but through children developing the ability to talk about their mathematical ideas in class – to express their thinking processes out loud while solving maths problems. Edwards argues that books and worksheets only provide children with symbols and pictures, and that alone, these learning tools cannot provide the full range of support for maths development. Children need the interactions of skilled and interested adults to ensure they have the practical experiences and conversation that are also crucial to learning maths.

The National Numeracy Strategy (NNS) supports this type of approach with more emphasis on oral work and less on written work. At Key Stage 1 the learning sequence is described as follows:

- Practical maths problems.

- Mental maths problems.

- Solving written maths problems.

This sequence effectively supports children's learning of maths from the concrete stage based on practical activities, which they may have become familiar with in the Foundation Stage, to being able to solve maths problems mentally, to writing down or solving written maths problems. How children move through this sequence should coincide with the development of their ability to write symbols and recognize their meaning.

3.2 Practical maths

In order to support children with maths, the children need to have practical experiences to begin to think mathematically and to understand how numbers work. Practical tasks help children understand the concepts underpinning mathematical operations, as described above. Children need to develop mental concepts about objects through practice of physically exploring them. Schmidt (1998: 69) argues that: 'No child is able to classify objects without a great deal of experience of exploring them using both his or her senses and physical exploration of objects.'

At a young age children start to learn about important relative concepts such as 'bigger' and 'smaller' and 'more' and 'fewer'. Practical tasks can help children become skilled and confident in their use of these concepts.

Tasks can include:

- Cooking which involves weighing, measuring and determining size.

- Sorting objects by different classifications, such as all the big objects and all the small objects, all the children with blue eyes and all the children with brown, sorting by colour, type and shape.

- Comparing objects and asking questions such as, 'Which is bigger?' or 'Which is the smallest?' Or longest or shortest.

- Practising estimation skills such as, 'Which cup will hold the most beads?' or, 'Who do you think is taller?'

- Sequencing a number of objects by a particular aspect such as length, height or width.

- Recognizing and repeating patterns.

Learning maths in abstract can be counter-productive for young children. For example, being able to count to ten in sequence does not have much value if the child cannot relate the number name to an actual number of objects. By practising counting real objects the child starts to recognize what 'five' or 'seven' really means, and what number names are actually for.

Sorting and matching activities are an important method of supporting children's growing understanding of patterns and relationships, which are significant in the development of mathematical thinking (Pound, 1999). It is important that these activities are part of this process and not isolated or unexplained.

The teaching assistant's role is often to support individual children or small groups to complete practical maths tasks. It is important to recognize that insisting on the children recording the outcomes is less important than helping them to understand the processes involved in the task. Children who struggle to understand the basic concepts described above may need to repeat the tasks until they grasp the meaning behind them and are confident to carry out the tasks themselves. Discussion and questioning is very important in terms of guiding children towards understanding. Questions can include asking children to estimate outcomes or to judge differences. For example:

- Which is bigger? (smaller, wider, shorter, longer, heavier)

- Which holds the most? (least, fewer, more)

- Who has got the most? (least, fewer, more)

- Who do you think will be tallest? (shortest, heaviest, lightest)

Children need to be encouraged to estimate outcomes without fear of being wrong. Mistakes can be useful in helping children understand the concepts being taught. Some children find it hard to be wrong and may become distressed if they make a mistake. Other may refuse to 'guess' in case they are wrong. You have an important role in encouraging children to take risks in estimating and to help them to consider why their estimates were different to the outcomes. Having the 'right' answer may not help a child understand how to solve the same type of problem in the future. Your role also includes reinforcing understanding in the wider range of contexts. For example, opportunities to ask and answer the questions outlined above (and many more) present themselves throughout the school day and across the curriculum.

A *chance to think*

Integrating the learning of maths across the school day can be an important part of helping children to become confident with basic concepts and to be able to estimate or predict outcomes. Children learn about mathematical concepts in a wide range of contexts in school and at home. Maths is part of daily life and when working with young children we need to be aware of, and exploit, opportunities which arise naturally to help children learn and use basic concepts. Conversation involving mathematical language has a crucial role in this process, helping children to build confidence and to ask questions. Children may also benefit from seeing tasks modelled so they can observe the process of working out a problem. However, practical tasks are the key to helping children to work out problems for themselves and absorb basic skills.

Exercise 4.1

Drawing from your own experience, list the different opportunities that arise across the whole school day, which support mathematical learning. Describe the contexts and opportunities you have come across, which can be used to help reinforce learning of mathematical concepts and language. Ask colleagues for their ideas. Compare your collection of ideas with those on page 165.

3.3 Mental maths

The *National Numeracy Strategy* emphasizes the development of mental maths and oral discussions of mathematical thinking as opposed to the early use of written maths problems. Hughes (1986) work was influential in our current understanding of how children learn about maths. He argued that young children can count without having actual objects in front of them – in essence, they can progress from the concrete understanding of maths processes developed through practical activities to mental maths. Children can learn to 'see' the objects to be counted in their heads when dealing with small numbers. For example, a child may be baffled by the request to add two and two, if his/her experience to date has been practical and concrete. However, he/she may be able to visualize two apples and add on two more apples because he/she has developed the ability to create mental images of the objects rather than having to see the objects in reality.

Pound (1999) suggests that number lines, hundred squares and other visual representations of numbers can help children to develop their skills in mental maths, as can structured apparatus such as Cuisenaire rods. *The National Numeracy Strategy Guide for Your Professional Development: Book 4* (DfEE, 1999b: 19) suggests that 'One of the most powerful images is the number line', and that

> Visualising the positions of numbers on the number line helps children to decide on an appropriate mental strategy. For example, when subtracting, children may decide that it is easier to count on from one number to the other (e.g. for calculations such as 84–78) or to count back the number they are subtracting (e.g. for calculations such as 84–6).

Conversations and discussions can also develop children's ability to make mental images of maths problems, as can counting on fingers. Laura, now 9, described this as 'first you count things that are there on the table, like bricks or whatever, and then you don't count the actual bricks but you can count them on your fingers in your head'. The development of mental maths can be supported by discussion with children which encourage them to articulate the ideas, skills and number facts they draw on during mental calculations which can then help them develop their strategies further (*The National Numeracy Strategy Guide for Your Professional Development: Book 4*, DfEE, 1999b).

3.4   Written maths

As discussed above, there is an emphasis at Key Stage 1 on oral and mental maths and on a range of recording methods – early mathematical mark-making which includes pictures, tally marks, pretend writing and symbols. It has already been mentioned above that a too early emphasis on conventional written maths work may put children off maths or confuse them completely.

However, eventually children will progress to the stage where they need to be able to write down maths problems using the conventional methods. This need to write maths problems down in the conventional way is precipitated by the increasing complexity of the calculations children are doing and the problems they may experience manipulating large numbers in their minds or trying to record them in pictures or icons. It is important that children go through a transition period, in which they can use familiar pictographs to record their work as well as conventional recording methods. They should be encouraged to use whatever method works and feels comfortable, until they have become confident in the use of conventional representation methods.

Anghileri's sequence of five steps can help children to develop conventional recording methods for maths problems (1995):

1. Children discuss their mathematical thinking with others.

2. Children show how they are thinking with objects or drawings.

3. Children start to record in some form.

4. Children are encouraged to use increasingly shorter forms of recording.

5. Children start to use standards forms of recording.

Children may have problems with reversing numbers when they first start to write them down, and they may also have difficulties remembering in which order numbers with more than one numeral are written e.g. writing 91 for 19. It is important to help children with these difficulties, but also to encourage the child to go back to earlier forms of representation if he/she is struggling with his/her understanding of written numbers.

4.   NUMBER AND COUNTING

The experience of counting is crucial to understanding number in the early years. Developing counting ability involves acquiring a range of skills and concepts, which the child must become confident with, in order to be able to count. Many of these are developed or developing before a child reaches school age, learned as part of their everyday experiences as discussed above. Edwards (1998: 27) comments that problems with counting and number recognition are associated with children 'whose early experiences have been severely limited'. The skills for counting have been classified as 'counting principles' (Gelman and Gallistel, 1978). They are:

- One-to-one principle – matching counting words to the items to be counted. Accuracy depends on ensuring that number words are said in order and that each item receives one number word tag. For example, when counting four bricks the child needs to be able to give each of the four items one number name only.

- Stable-order principle – number names and numerals are in a fixed order. Accuracy depends on learning the permanence of the order of number names and numerals. For example, when counting four bricks the child needs always to count one, two, three and four in the same order.

- Cardinality of numbers – the last number names the set and indicates the size of the set. Accuracy depends on being able to apply the one-to-one principle and the stable-order principle.

- Abstraction principle – applying the skill of counting to any set of objects. Accuracy depends on the child's ability to count same and mixed sets of objects. For example, the child will know that four objects will always be counted as four whether they are bricks or balls, or a mixture.

- Order-irrelevance principle – the order in which a set of objects is counted does not influence the amount. The cardinal number of the set remains the same, whatever the order of counting. The number tags given to objects during a particular count only apply for that count. For example, if the red brick is number three on one count, this does not mean it has to be number three on the next count.

Children also use a strategy called subitizing, which allows them to recognize the cardinal number of a small number of objects without counting them individually. Subitizing works up to about six, hence some children's ability to recognize the numbers on the face of a dice during board games, without counting each time (Warren and Westmoreland, 2000).

O'Hara (2000) advises that there are many opportunities for children to count and develop skills for counting in the daily life of a school. Children need to count many different types of things to develop counting skills. These could include movements, sounds, objects and incidents of a particular event, such as how often a word appears in a rhyme or poem.

A chance to think

Counting is crucial to progress in maths and children need to be able to grasp the principles underpinning counting (outlined above) in order to be able to count. Many children start to learn to count at an early age, supported by parents who count steps as they walk down them, count bricks as they construct with them and give number names to sets ('two biscuits') wherever possible.

> ## Exercise 4.2
>
> During one day at school, note the range of opportunities to count which could be used to support the development of counting skills for one class. How many of these opportunities were taken up? How could they be used to support children who struggle with counting correctly? Try and think of ways of building more counting practice into the day, including opportunities to learn about counting through play. Compare your ideas with those of a colleague or your mentor.

Developing an understanding of number also involves a range of skills and concepts. Many of these are dependent on accurate counting skills. These principles are:

- Ordering – the concept of quantity and how that is recorded. Distinguishing between different numbers by name, which are recorded as numerals. Accuracy depends on understanding the concept of 'as many as' and recognizing the fixed order of numbers.

- Making comparisons – comparing the order relationship between sets with different cardinal numbers. For example, that a set of five is bigger than a set of four. Accuracy depends on being able to demonstrate understanding of 'more' and 'fewer'. For example, being able to put sets of one, two, three, and four objects in order and to answer questions correctly about which sets have more or fewer objects in relation to each other.

- Addition and subtraction – this follows on from making comparisons. It involves recognizing that the cardinal number increases as the quantity of items in a set increase. Accuracy depends on learning ordinal numbers and finger counting and the concept of 0.

4.1 Common errors with number and counting

Children make the same common errors in number and counting, many of them related to one-to-one inaccuracies. For example, touching but not counting, counting twice, not counting an object at all, counting out of sequence (missing a counting name), not understanding zero. Edwards (1998: 30) also notes that children may have problems learning to count-on when adding sets of numbers. For example, a child may fail to understand when adding up her two sets of fingers, that she can count-on from five when adding on the second hand. In order to subtract, children need to be able to count backwards as well as forwards.

5. SHAPE, SPACE AND MEASURES

Learning about shape, space and measures lends itself to a wide range of practical activities and investigations. For example, modelling in different materials is one way in which children can be supported to recognize the dimensions and properties of different shapes. Pound (1999: 40) suggests that children may find it easier to learn about three-dimensional shapes before they start on two-dimensional representations: 'The physical form of three-dimensional shapes allows children to gain a better understanding of what two-dimensional are since faces and sides are easily identifiable.'

Handling objects of different shapes, exploring size and shape through practical activities and discussing their views are all important aspects of development in this area. Children can measure a wide range of different objects or quantities using different measuring techniques and instruments. Edwards (1998: 156) states: 'They need to be actively involved in measuring, balancing, pouring and timing games using arbitrary and standard units, if skill of estimation and accuracy in measuring are to be developed.'

Children should be encouraged to use a whole range of measuring methods in order to understand the process of measurement. These should include standard measures such as rulers or tape measures as well as non-standard measures such as 'this room is the length of five pupils lying in a line'. When using standard measures children need to start to understand how these relate to each other e.g. there are 1000 centimetres in a metre, and they need to practise estimating lengths so that they get a clear idea of what a metre and a centimetre are in length.

The National Numeracy Strategy Guidance for Your Professional Development: Book 4 (DfEE, 1999b) suggests that children need to develop a very clear understanding of the language of size, shape and space in order to achieve in this area. Precise use of terms such as 'bigger', 'taller', wider' can help children understand the different aspects of an object they are measuring. Ebbutt and Taylor (2001) suggest that children may be confused by the mathematical meanings of everyday words, and therefore this is an area where care must be taken to ensure children are clear in their understanding. Describing the differences between shapes and objects can be very useful in helping children understand the language of different dimensions. Looking at shape in the environment can support learning in this area as can construction, modelling and other creative activities.

Measuring volume through water activities can be particularly enjoyable for children, and can be very positive in developing concepts such as 'more than' and 'less than'. Children should always be encouraged to estimate measurement so that they start to understand different standard units.

6. THE TEACHING ASSISTANT'S ROLE

In the light of the discussion above, it is clear that there is a real need for a high level of support for children learning maths at Key Stage 1. Transforming their early practice-based ideas and understanding of maths into a more abstract type of knowledge, which is recorded symbolically, is quite a task for young children. As such, teaching assistants have a clear role supporting mathematical learning in the classroom.

Determining the teaching assistant's specific role should be part of the planning process involving the teacher and yourself. However, the *National Numeracy Strategy: Framework for Teaching Mathematics* outlines the general role of classroom assistants in teaching and learning of maths (DfEE, 1999a: 24).

Emphasis is placed on the teaching assistant's role in:

- **Supporting individual pupils during whole class teaching** This can be achieved by sitting with a child and prompting him/her to speak; reminding him/her to listen; using checking questions to be sure he/she has understood; indicating to the teacher that he/she may have a point to make.

- **Assessing the needs of children they will be supporting through observation during whole class teaching**. Observing and noting the areas in which the children show lack of understanding or low levels of skill, throughout the taught session; recognizing that all small group and individual support work must be based on a good understanding of the children's level of achievement to date, prior knowledge and experience and areas of concern.

- **Working with groups**. Working with groups of children to support their progress and to ensure that they have understood what is required; helping more able children to extend their work; helping less able children to reach the highest standard they can achieve by reviewing earlier principles, giving concrete examples, breaking the process down into smaller steps, and encouraging the children to talk through their thinking processes; giving praise and encouragement; helping the teacher by developing and delivering differentiated work as agreed.

- **Working with individual children**. Supporting children with specific needs in maths or more general learning delays or special educational needs by working with the child; helping him/her to stay on task; reminding the child of earlier principles; breaking the work down into smaller tasks; encouraging the child to talk about his/her processes; giving praise and encouragement.

Teaching assistants have an important role in feeding back information to the teacher about children's progress and ability; any problems individual children may have; the effectiveness of the session in meeting the teaching objectives, and any suggestions for future sessions. There is a format for recording this feedback in *The Teaching Assistant's File* (DfEE, 2000) in section 7, and some example maths activities that are useful for new teaching assistants to look at.

Perhaps one of the most difficult aspects of supporting children in Key Stage 1 maths is that there is a multitude of ways of solving maths problems and this can be both confusing and cause uncertainty among adults. Children will develop different ways of solving maths problems and these will differ between different children. Edwards (1998: 24) discusses the range of methods children use to solve maths problems and how these are more likely to link to the child's practical experiences of maths than their 'book-taught maths'. Children will use a range of different approaches for solving maths problems, and as long as these are based on effective principles and they work, then it is important not to try and standardize the child's methods. Edwards (1998: 26) states that: 'The ways in which children learn mathematics cannot be generalised into a universal formula. Whilst there are common principles, the active process of learning is dynamic and idiosyncratic.'

A *chance to think*

It can seem uncomfortable at times to work with children who are using a range of maths methods that vary significantly. You, and possibly the parents, may ask whether there is a single, 'right' way of approaching a specific type of maths problem. Although some methods are going to be easier than others, and some less effective, essentially there are many variations on the ways in which maths problems can be solved, and most of these have value. Children will use the methods that make sense to them and work for them.

Exercise 4.3

Look at the maths problems below and solve them in your head. Then for each problem, write down exactly how you solved it i.e. the steps or processes you went through to get the right answer. For example, you could subtract 147 from 200 by taking 150 from 200 and then adding 3, the difference between 47 and 50. Or you could take 7 from 0, carrying 1 over to make it 7 from 10, pay the 1 back, carry another 1 over and take 5 from 10, pay the one back and take 2 from 2. The answer is the same, the methods are different.

Ask a few colleagues or friends to go through the same exercise, without showing them your notes. Compare the methods used to get the answers. Did everyone use the same approach? How many approaches were used? Did they all work effectively to reach the correct solution?

$397 - 284 = ?$
$452 + 139 = ?$
$1020 - 350 = ?$
$129 - 45 = ?$

If a child solves a maths problem incorrectly, it is important not just to correct it, but instead to talk through the processes involved with the child so that he/she can see where his/her calculation went astray. 'Wrong' answers can be good learning experiences for children and should be treated as such, rather than as a failure on the child's part. The teaching assistant may get more insight into the child's mental processes through incorrect solutions than through correct ones. The teaching assistant can perhaps contribute most by talking to children about maths and how maths problems can be solved, and encouraging children to discuss their own thinking out loud. By talking about their own mathematical thinking children will start to feel more certain of how to tackle maths problems. This process does not need to be confined to the numeracy hour – talking through all your mathematical problem-solving will help children to understand how you reach your answers and will help them adopt this approach themselves. For example, any collections of money are a good opportunity to add up different amounts out loud.

Adults who talk about how they solve maths problems are good role models and can be crucial in supporting the development of this approach in children. It is important, however, to be clear that your approach is not the only one and not necessarily the 'best' one. Using mathematical language and helping children to understand the meaning of different terms is also important. Children need to become used to different terms and know what they mean. They need to relate these terms to mathematical symbols and be confident in their understanding of these.

Teaching assistants can also help draw the lines between different maths experiences children have, so that their learning is 'of a piece' and makes sense to them. Through discussion, demonstration and reminding children of previous activities, teaching assistants can help children draw on existing learning as a basis for new learning. Knowing the child's level of achievement and previous experiences is very important in this process.

6.1 Differentiation and children with additional needs

Differentiating maths to suit a large mixed ability class is quite a challenge. The role of the teaching assistant can be crucial in ensuring that groups and individual children get support as required. It is important to be sure what the goals of a differentiated task are, so that all children reach the minimum levels of achievement within the task. Edwards (1998: 210) suggests a model of three levels of expectations to cover different levels of ability:

- Minimum – what every child should know and understand by the end of the teaching session.

- Optimum – what most children will know and understand.

- Extension – what some children will know and understand.

The teaching assistant should be sure of which of these levels a group or individual child is working towards, and what the 'bottom line' is in terms of minimum levels of performance in a particular session.

Children with learning delays or special educational needs may need to develop their maths work at a slower rate than other children do. Because maths is in general a subject where new learning has to be based on existing foundations, some children may need to 'go back' and strengthen their understanding of those earlier areas of knowledge, before they can tackle the next stage. One of the roles of the teaching assistant is to recognize and respond to children who are having problems with a new concept because of a poor grasp of a previous concept. Some children may also have difficulties in reading written instructions and will need support to understand what the task is.

Some children may need tasks broken down into more steps than others to help them understand the task. For example, the child may need to consciously think about the meaning of the =, + or − signs as part of their working through a maths problem, if they are not completely sure of the meaning of these symbols. If a child is baffled by the task, introducing a practical activity to demonstrate the new concept may help him gain firmer understanding of the principles involved.

CONCLUSIONS

The role of teaching assistants in supporting mathematical development is crucial. Children develop their mathematical thinking at different rates, and many need support in moving from practical aspects to more abstract aspects of maths. Key issues for consideration are ensuring there is a good link between children's early experience and their Key Stage 1 activities. Teaching assistants have a central role in observing and responding to children who have failed to understand earlier concepts and are not able to engage in the current learning because of this.

Using the language of maths precisely and supporting children's learning by modelling and encouraging 'thinking out loud' are also key roles. Children need support at times to review earlier stages of learning and even return to concrete practical demonstrations to help their understanding. Relating maths to everyday events and drawing on environmental numbers, shapes, measures and calculations can be very useful in making maths 'real' to children. Above all, teaching assistants can support children in their transition to maths in school by generating enthusiasm for the subject and confidence in their approach to it.

NOTES FOR FURTHER READING

Anghileri, J. (1995)
Children's Mathematical Thinking in the Early Years: Perspectives on Children's Learning.
London: Cassell.

Department for Education and Science (DES) (1982)
Mathematics Counts (Cockcroft Report).
London: HMSO.

DfEE (1999a)
National Numeracy Strategy: Framework for Teaching Mathematics.
Nottingham: DfEE.

DfEE (1999b)
The National Numeracy Strategy Guide for Your Professional Development: Book 4.
Nottingham: DfEE.

DfEE (2000)
The Teaching Assistant's File.
Nottingham: DfEE.

DfEE/QCA (1999)
National Curriculum for England and Wales – Mathematics, www.nc.uk.net
Nottingham: DfEE.

Ebbutt, S. and Taylor, J. (2001)
'Talking Maths'
TES Primary, February, 27–38.

Edwards, S. (1998)
Managing Effective Teaching of Mathematics 3–8.
London: Paul Chapman.

Gelman, R. and Gallistel, C. R. (1978)
The *Child's Understanding of Number.*
New York: Harvard University Press.

Griffiths, R. (1994)
'Mathematics and Play', Chapter 12 in Moyles, J. (ed.) *The Excellence of Play*.
Milton Keynes: Open University Press.

Haylock, D. and Cockburn, A. (1997)
Understanding Mathematics in the Lower Primary Years.
London: Paul Chapman.

Hughes, M. (1986)
Children and Number.
Oxford: Basil Blackwell.

Munn, P. and Schaffer, H. R. (1993)
'Literacy and numeracy events in social interactive contexts'.
International Journal of Early Years Education, 1(3), 61–80.

O'Hara, M. (2000)
Teaching 3–8 – Meeting the Standards for Initial Teacher Training and Induction.
London: Continuum.

Pound, L. (1999)
Supporting Mathematical Development in the Early Years.
Milton Keynes: Open University Press.

Qualifications and Curriculum Authority (QCA) (2000)
Curriculum Guidance for the Foundation Stage.
Sudbury: QCA.

Schmidt, S. (1998)
A Guide to Early Years Practice.
London: Routledge.

Warren, V. and Westmoreland, S. (2000)
'Number in play and everyday life'. Chapter 16 in Drury, R., Miller, L. and
Campbell, R. (eds. *Looking at Early Years Education and Care*)
London: David Fulton.

CHAPTER 5

Supporting Key Stage 1 Science

Science is such an integrated feature of so many aspects of our everyday life, that in some respects we take many aspects of science and products of scientific endeavour for granted. Yet, although we are interested in and curious about science, this 'goes hand-in-hand with a deep-seated fear of and hostility towards it' (Wolpert, 1993 cited in Newton, 2000). Candidates for teacher training in the primary sector now have to have a GCSE in science at grade C or above to qualify for a place on the course. For some other staff supporting science in schools and nursery, there may be real fears about how to approach what can seem a daunting and unfriendly subject. Images of men in white coats in laboratories, standing in front of chalkboards filled with incomprehensible mathematical equations, viewed across a bank of bubbling test tubes, spring to mind.

There is an equality issue here as well, with many studies demonstrating that girls and children from ethnic minorities are disadvantaged in the sciences. In terms of gender, Siraj-Blatchford and MacLeod Brudenell (1999: 38) suggest that: 'Mothers, older sisters, aunts and grandmothers may not have provided the kind of positive scientific role models that brother, uncles, fathers and grandfathers have.' Many teaching assistants are female and there is a real opportunity to work towards redressing this balance, through sharing meaningful and relevant scientific explorations with young children. In terms of cultural differences, Holland and Rowan (1996: 10) suggest that the science curriculum should include cross-cultural links such as food, celebrations, languages and the scientific achievements of a range of cultures, in order to combat the stereotype of white, male scientists, which still has much influence on our children. For example, topics about humans and how we grow and change can sensitively address these issues and reinforce the similarities between people rather than the relatively superficial differences.

In this age of rapid technological development, new scientific discoveries and applications of scientific knowledge are a daily event. Children grow up regarding the results of scientific exploration and application as a natural part of their world. Yet children also have a desire to explore the world around them for themselves and to work out the questions that occur to them such as, 'How does it work?' and, 'What happens if?'.

The idea of children as 'natural explorers', who will seek explanations for the things they see and experience in their environments, is one that is commonly held. Bloomfield *et al.* (2000: 149) state that: 'We are explorers from the cradle to the grave. We seem to be born with curiosity, "a need to know".' However, Siraj-Blatchford and MacLeod Brudenell (1999) argue that although children may be natural scientists they need guidance to ensure that what they find out about the world around them is accurate. Otherwise, they may reach conclusions about events in their environment, which are basically incorrect.

Harlen (2000: 57) suggests the following may occur and lead to misconceptions:

- Children take account of only some factors that are relevant.

- Things are considered from only one point of view, their own.

- Inappropriate links are made.

- Predictions may be no more than stating what is already known, so that they are bound to be confirmed.

- Evidence may be selectively used to support an existing idea, ignoring what may be in contradiction.

Examples of these misconceptions include children who believe that objects float or sink because of their colour; that bigger objects will sink because of their size; that ice melts because it is placed in a drink, not because of changes in temperature.

A chance to think

Children's misconceptions about science may come from a variety of sources, some of them stemming from the child's own immature understanding and some from the child making assumptions based on links which are not relevant. For example, a child may believe that because some liquids can become solids (such as glue) then remain as solids under normal conditions, then this will apply to all liquids that can become solids. Many young children believe that you can 'save' ice or snow as solids. They may also misunderstand the factors that lead to melting and not recognize that the cause is heat. Children need to be encouraged to test their assumptions and rethink their ideas in order to reach more accurate conclusions.

Exercise 5.1

Observe children in science activities in class and make notes on common misconceptions they hold.

What are the misconceptions based on?

What sort of help could be given to the children to reach better understanding? Discuss your conclusions and suggestions with a colleague or mentor.

It is important to encourage an enquiring mind and to help children formulate and ask questions about their environment. Children need to know that scientific enquiry does not take place in a vacuum. It is part of an ongoing and developing body of knowledge, understanding, developments and applications that is part of the past, present and future.

Newton (2000) suggests three aspects to scientific enterprise:

- Science as a product – the existing body of scientific knowledge.

- Science as a process – the development of skills to achieve a scientific approach to enquiry.

- Science as people – science is 'done' by people and scientific enterprise has relevance to our lives.

(Adapted from Newton, 2000: 14)

Scientific knowledge must always be viewed in the context of what is already known in the particular area of enquiry. As such, many major scientific findings are based on the development and growth of a body of knowledge, drawing on the work of a range of contributors who constantly develop and refine what is known through their work. When children learn about science, it is important for them to have knowledge of the existing body of scientific knowledge and the outcomes of previous investigations and breakthroughs in order to develop an understanding of the concept of a scientific community with a shared body of scientific knowledge.

Young children need to learn through first-hand experiences (see Chapter 2), so although much of science is developed through mathematical theory-testing, in the early years there is a strong emphasis on children being involved in experimentation and investigation through 'doing'.

Therefore, science education in the early years is developed on the following principles:

- Children need to do experiments in order to learn about science in a practical way.

- Children need to learn that the scientific knowledge we have is a result of experimentation and the development of theory to explain the outcomes of experimentation.

- Children need to learn the 'rules' of developing scientific knowledge through rigorous testing of theories and analysis of findings.

- Children need to know that all their own and others' work on science takes place in the context of existing scientific knowledge.

- Learning about the way that scientific knowledge has developed over time helps children to understand why and how we do science now.

However, Harlen (2000: 46) also states that there are a number of attitudes, which children need to develop for learning science. These attitudes are:

- Curiosity – 'I want to know!'

- Respect for evidence – 'Prove it!'

- Willingness to change ideas – in response to evidence

- Critical reflection – 'It would have worked better if . . . .'

- Sensitivity towards living things and the environment.

The last point is closely connected to the growth of ethical approaches to scientific investigation, which take into account the impact of humans on the environment and their responsibilities towards protecting that environment. Harlen argues that children develop more mature attitudes in each of these areas over time, but that this development is uneven between children of the same age. It is important to recognize these differences in developmental stages and to take them into account when supporting individual children. As with all learning, the experiences that children have in school will build on and complement the learning that takes place within or through the home environment.

1. LEARNING ABOUT SCIENCE AT HOME

Children are learning about science all the time, from when they discover the power of gravity by pushing their lunch off the highchair tray (an experiment many babies go on to repeat in true scientific fashion!), to learning about the growth of plants through gardening, the properties of different materials through handling and manipulating, and the ways in which so many of the products of science and technology support our lives. Young children learn about science in the home through:

- Observations of objects and events around them.

- Conversations and explanations shared with adults or other children.

- Their own practical experiments.

For example, Laura, at the age of 5, was making Christmas biscuits, which were iced with green and red icing. She was fascinated at the way in which the white icing sugar melted and changed when mixed with water, and then changed again when mixed with the different food colourings. She experimented with different amounts of the colour in water to see how much was needed to get different shades and depths of colour. She then mixed the colours together to see what different colours she could get, and also tried mixing the icing with different amounts of water to get different consistencies. Laura's experiments were guided by an adult who:

- Shared the experiments with her.

- Made suggestions as to different mini-experiments.

- Encouraged her to predict what may happen.

- Asked questions about what was happening and why.

- Encouraged her to ask questions about what was happening and why.

- Suggested how the experiments with colour could be extended to different materials such as paint.

The role of the adult was important in shaping and supporting the learning that was taking place, and ensuring the experiments did not deteriorate into chaos.

In order to develop an enquiring mind, young children need to have opportunities for exploration, play and experimentation at home, with the guidance and support of adults who will role model a questioning approach and support the process of enquiry. Children who do not have these experiences may find it more difficult to get involved in scientific enquiry at a later stage.

Common experiences at home can include:

- Cooking – the effect of mixing different ingredients; the changes which take place when heat is applied.

- Artwork – mixing paints, glues and solids, like paper or clay, with water; mixing different colours; painting on different surfaces.

- Gardening – growing plants from seeds or bulbs; making compost; experimenting with the light, heat and water needs of different plants.

- Mini-creatures – exploring the outside world for small creatures and observing their behaviour and appearance.

- Seasonal change – observing and talking about the changes in plant and animal life, daylight and nightfall, the temperature and weather.

- Caring for pets – observing the behaviour and habits of pets; discussing their needs and requirements; visiting the vet; feeding and watering.

These are only a tiny example of the multitude of everyday experiences many children have, which support their scientific learning at home and the development of their capacity to enquire.

However, children who have limited early experiences because of socioeconomic deprivations or family or parenting problems may have little access to the early learning of science, which is based on the exploration of the world around them. For example, a 5-year-old, who had limited experiences due to the quality of her early parenting, was taken to a pretty Peak District dale by her new adoptive parents. 'What is this?' she asked. 'Cows, trees, river?' tried her mum. 'No! This!' spreading her arms wide. 'The countryside,' replied her mum, recognizing at last that her daughter had never even seen the country in books, never mind the 'real thing'. In the child's reception class report one month later, her teacher commented on the 'massive gaps in her understanding of the physical and natural world'. This anecdote reminds us that we should never make assumptions about the level and extent of a child's knowledge on entry to school. Knowledge and understanding of science will be shaped by the child's social and economic circumstances, parenting experiences, culture and religion and the specific learning the child has had access to in the past.

A chance to think

In Chapter 2, the ways in which young children learn best are discussed and one of the conclusions drawn is that children need to integrate their learning in the home with the learning that takes place in school, in order to continue the process of constructing their own understanding of their world.

Exercise 5.2

Look at the list above and try and consider how the activities which children are involved in at school build on these (and other) early experiences.

How do we assess what children already know?

What sort of support do we give to children with limited early experiences?

How are activities structured to help children make links between their different experiences?

Discuss your conclusions with a colleague or mentor.

2. SCIENCE IN THE FOUNDATION STAGE 3 TO 5 YEARS

One of the areas of learning within the *Curriculum Guidance for the Foundation Stage* (QCA, 2000) is 'knowledge and understanding of the world' which provides a basis for learning science within the National Curriculum, among other subjects. The guidance emphasizes the role of:

- First-hand experiences.

- Activities which will stimulate children's interest and curiosity.

- Opportunities for children to learn about their own and others' unique identities.

- Learning to talk about and record what they find out.

- Additional support for children with sensory impairment.

As with all the learning activities in the Foundation Stage, it is important to build on children's early learning experiences in their homes. The concept of the Bruner's spiral curriculum can be useful in helping us to understand the link between different stages of children's scientific learning. The spiral curriculum suggests that children can learn about any aspect of their world at any stage, but that their learning is more simple or complex depending on their stage of development. Children will revisit the same topics at different stages of their development, adding to and extending their existing knowledge and understanding. In this way, earlier learning experiences form the basis of later learning experiences.

For example, Amy, as a young infant, learned through experience that ice comes out of the freezer as a solid and then becomes liquid. She learned the word 'melt' to describe this process. She also learned that if we want to have more ice, we must put water into the freezer. Amy also noticed that when the lava lamp (an enclosed glass lamp with wax moving in different shapes through coloured liquid) was lit, the wax divided into small shapes and rose to the top of the liquid, and then fell back down towards the bulb. This pattern was constantly repeated. When the lamp was off, however, the wax lay in a solid lump at the bottom of the liquid. Through questioning, she came to understand that the heat of the light bulb melted the wax and that it floated when it was hotter. As it reached the top of the liquid, furthest away from the heat, it cooled and sank back towards the bulb, and the pattern was repeated. When the lamp was off the cold wax was heavier than the liquid. Amy was able to incorporate this more sophisticated understanding of the behaviour of liquids and solids into her existing understanding. She already knew that substances could be liquid or solid and that heat had a role in this change sometimes, and therefore, could build her more complex understanding on this basis.

Observation of the child's play and response to activities are important in assessing individual children's levels of experience and understanding of the natural and material world. Children need to learn a range of skills for exploration, as well as new knowledge and understanding. In the Foundation Stage skills, knowledge and understanding are developed mainly through practical activities, which form the basis of learning and support children in building confidence in their own explorations. Riley and Savage (1994: 136) state that: 'The early years classroom that naturally employs an enquiry-based explorative model of teaching and learning has great potential for science.'

For example, Dan, aged 4, wanted to find out about small creatures living on or near a local pond. He had seen insects skating across the top of the pond and wanted to find out more. He discussed his ideas with an adult, and decided a visit to the pond was a 'good idea'. He wanted to catch the insects in a transparent container so he could observe them. He chose a plastic box with a lid, but was worried the insects would suffocate. With help, he made holes with a needle in the plastic box. He also made an insect-catcher from a small cup and piece of card, using scissors, under supervision, to cut card to the right size to slide under the cup when an insect was captured. Dan took a notebook and felt-tips and a magnifying glass to the pond (and a torch in case of the sudden onset of nightfall!). He captured some small creatures, with help, and transferred them to his box. He examined them through his magnifying glass and made marks to record their behaviour and pictures to record their appearance. He shared his experiences with the other children and the adult through discussion about the creatures and how they behaved, and a commentary on the success of his planning and preparation for the activity.

The adult role was to discuss how plans could be made and put into practice and to help with practical aspects and safety issues. The adults also supported a sense of excitement and anticipation and asked questions about the process and outcome of the investigation. In this way, the adult encouraged Dan to predict e.g. 'How many legs will this one have?' and to review the investigation e.g. 'What worked, what could have been done differently, what did we find out?'.

First-hand experiences give children the opportunity to develop their own understanding, building on their experiences at home. Activities need to relate to the knowledge and understanding children already have, in order to make sense for them. For example, Dan, when 3, enjoyed making models out of mashed-up wet painted paper. He gradually learned through experimentation that although putting paint on the paper gave it some 'body', in fact, paint is not a good adhesive for holding models in shape. He absorbed this new knowledge and then sought different ways of sticking the paper together. He tried sticky tape and was happy with the strength of the shape, but not with the fact that paint does not stick to the tape. Through experimentation with different adhesives, he 'invented' a mixture of paint and glue, which allowed him to model in the way he wanted to.

Riley and Savage (1994: 139) refer to this as 'open-ended problem-solving through practical activities'. O'Hara (2000: 31) suggests that early first-hand experiences can prepare children for Key Stage 1 Science by helping children to develop a range of skills including:

- Critical thinking (asking questions about why and how things happen, predicting).

- Problem-solving and investigating.

- Observational skills.

- Measuring, sorting and classifying.

- Hypothesizing (talking about their observations, identifying cause and effect).

These skills can be developed through a range of practical activities in the

Foundation Stage, supported by adults who consolidate and clarify learning through conversation and questioning.

3. THE ROLE OF ADULTS

Siraj-Blatchford and MacLeod Brudenell (1999) argue that adults need to become active role models to young children, exploring and investigating the world with them and acknowledging the widespread existence of science. They need to role-model observational skills, investigation skills and effective methods of enquiry. Adults also have a very important role in clarifying and extending the children's knowledge and understanding, reversing misconceptions and making sense of outcomes. Without adult guidance, children may reach understandable, but incorrect, conclusions about their discoveries. For example, children in a nursery class were choosing and placing different objects in water to see which floated and which did not. By coincidence, the large objects floated and the smaller objects sank, leading the children to start to believe that this would always be the case. The parent helper suggested a few more trials and quietly introduced some objects, which she knew would reverse the trend, to 'head-off' the mistaken conclusion the children were about to reach.

Conversation with children can be used to develop and refine ideas, and to help them produce a sequence of small steps towards achieving their desired goals. For example, when Dan was planning his trip to the pond, he shared his ideas about how to conduct his experiments with the adult, and between them they established a simple sequence of activities with which to complete the investigation. Through this discussion, Dan's plans became clearer and more achievable. The adult also asked questions and made suggestions to extend Dan's understanding and areas of investigation. Conversation was a crucial part of the process of completing the investigation and reaching conclusions.

Bloomfield *et al.* (2000) suggest that adult questions can stimulate children's enquiry in the following areas:

- Observation – what do you notice? What do you see?

- Classification – what does it remind you of? Which are the same as each other?

- Predictions – what will happen next? What will happen if?

- Testing – how can we find out? Shall we do it again? Shall we change anything?

(Adapted from Bloomfield et al., 2000: 150)

A chance to think

Siraj-Blatchford and MacLeod Brudenell (1999: 18) refer to the 'talk cycle' as a model for good quality responsive conversation with children. The cycle is:

- Listen to the child – take what she or he says seriously.

- Try to understand what they mean.

- Use the child's meaning as the basis for the next adult comment, remark, suggestion, or question.

- Try to speak or act in a way that the child understands.

In this way, the conversation becomes based on the child's views, perceptions and opinions, not the adult's. This approach can not only help the child in her learning, but it can also help the adult to assess the child's level of knowledge and understanding more effectively and accurately.

Exercise 5.3

Try out the 'talk cycle' with a child or children during a practical science activity.
　What learning was taking place?
　In what ways did your conversation with the child or children contribute to this?
　Discuss your findings with a colleague or mentor.

Riley and Savage (1994: 139) argue that adult involvement is important to guide children where multiple solutions present themselves, particularly if the child lacks confidence. 'Open-ended enquiry' can seem daunting if a myriad of different answers present themselves. Children may need support to structure their approach and make sense of what they find. They may also need support to feel able to make mistakes, try out new experiments and draw reasonable conclusions from these. Adult involvement is also important in developing the language of science, teaching children new words to describe the things they are observing or making happen through their own activities. Recording of experiments or investigations can be supported through diagrams and pictures, mark-making and emergent writing, although O'Hara (2000) points out that formal recording may not be desirable or necessary with younger children, and concentrating on conversation may be more useful on some occasions.

Adults also have a role in promoting an interest in and enthusiasm for developing knowledge and understanding of the world, by drawing children's attention to aspects of the natural and manufactured environment, and discussing how it could be explored further.

Questioning and conversation have a key role in helping children to gain knowledge, reach understanding and apply their skills in science and across the curriculum. However, Brown and Wragg (1993: 18) sound a cautionary note about the way that adults question children, suggesting a number of common errors:

- Asking too many questions at once.

- Asking a question and answering it yourself.

- Asking a difficult question too early.

- Asking irrelevant questions.

- Asking the same type of questions.

- Not using probing questions.

- Not correcting wrong answers.

- Failing to see the implications of answers.

- Failing to build on answers.

It is important to consider the questions that are asked and the value they have and to ensure that they are appropriate to the child and to the context. Timing is important too – it is very important not to interrupt children's work to ask questions that may seem to be an annoying distraction, rather than a tool for progressing the learning process.

3.1 Safe science

Adult involvement is crucial in ensuring that the learning process of scientific experimentation in the early years is conducted safely. Adults should model safe use of tools and equipment, such as scissors, magnifying glasses, magnets, liquids, solids and adhesives and paint. They must help children to understand the dangers of electricity, heat and sharp instruments. Learning how to use instruments safely and effectively is an important part of scientific learning in both the Foundation Stage and at Key Stage 1, and can help and support children in planning and executing specific activities. The adult role in safe science can include:

- Monitoring children carefully during scientific experiments, especially those which involve sharp tools, heat or potentially toxic liquids.

- Helping children to hold and use instruments properly and safely.

- Reminding children not to drink liquids in experiments.

- Ensure hand-washing after handling any creatures, large or small, or any potentially toxic liquids or solids or before cooking or handling food.

- Cleaning equipment and surfaces after cooking or other activities.

- Reminding children about the dangers of mains electricity.

- Promoting an atmosphere of quiet but concentrated enquiry.

- Being aware of any allergies or medical problems individual children may have.

The teaching assistant may have a specific role in particular activities in helping children to complete these safely and carefully to achieve good results. For example, when cooking with children the teaching assistant may need to ensure that they wash their hands and work surfaces before starting, that they do not taste raw ingredients, that hair and clothes are kept out of the food, and that they clean up properly afterwards. Classroom management for safety needs to be part of joint planning between the teacher and teaching assistant to ensure that the classroom is set out in a safe way for the particular activity. General points include:

- Keeping the classroom tidy and free of clutter during science activities.

- Ensuring there are regular checks on all groups for safety reasons.

- Reminding children of safety hazards on frequent occasions.

- Ensuring children with learning difficulties or sensory impairments have extra support.

Children will also need safety support during trips out, which may include nature walks or other explorations of the environment. The teacher will make safety arrangements within school and LEA guidelines, and your role will be to ensure these arrangements are put into practice. These may include:

- Checking numbers of children at frequent intervals.

- Maintaining safety on the roads, especially when children are walking.

- Ensuring children are appropriately dressed for the trip.

- Promoting and maintaining quiet orderly behaviour.

- Dealing with any illness or distress.

- Ensuring any parent volunteer helpers are aware of safety guidelines.

- Communicating any problems to the teacher.

A *chance to think*

Teaching assistants have a significant role in supporting safe practice in science, in collaboration with the class teacher. Safe practice is crucial in ensuring that children enjoy science activities without suffering harm and also that they develop good practices for later, more complex science activities. However, young children can quickly forget safety rules, especially if the activity is exciting or absorbing, and therefore adults need to be vigilant in order to ensure safety standards remain high.

Exercise 5.4

During a science activity, consider the safety issues that arise and the safe practices you are required to follow. Make a note of these afterwards and then consider if all safety issues were included in the planning of the activity.
Are there safety guidelines within the school?
What sort of discussions did you have with the teacher about safety?
How are newly appointed support staff inducted into safe practices in science activities in the classroom?
Discuss your ideas with a colleague or mentor.

---

4. | LEARNING SCIENCE THROUGH PLAY

Learning science through play in the early years is a fascinating opportunity for both children and adults. Children can experiment with the properties of an enormous range of materials, they can discover information about living things, large and small, and they can do this through the safe and familiar medium of play, where mistakes do not matter and new investigations can build on existing knowledge. Adults can observe children at play and learn about individual children's levels of knowledge and understanding of the natural and material world. They can use this understanding as a basis for structured activities, or to correct misconceptions through conversation or other investigations.

Riley and Savage (1994: 136) use Hutt's model of epistemic (exploratory) play and ludic (sociodramatic, imaginative) play to explore the role of play in learning science in the early years. In this model, children learn about new aspects of their environment through exploration and add this new knowledge to their existing perceptions and understanding of their world. Imaginative play then gives children the opportunity to consolidate and become familiar with the application of their new knowledge and ideas.

For example, Laura, at 5, wanted to have a rabbit as a pet. She read stories about rabbits with her family, and went to the local children's farm where she was allowed to hold and stroke a rabbit and a guinea pig. She asked some questions and found out that rabbits and guinea pigs have different habits and needs. Laura had a lot of soft toy animals, including a rabbit and a guinea pig. She and her friend made a children's animal farm and 'looked after' their animals according to their specific needs and habits, giving them suitable habitats and 'food'. From this play, they started to extend and consolidate their knowledge and understanding of the needs and behaviour of different small animals, and they began to learn about the responsibilities of caring for a pet. From these experiences, Laura decided that looking after small animals is hard work, and she was going to wait until she was 8 to have a rabbit!

The adult role was to provide opportunities for first-hand experiences and to structure those experiences so that they make sense to the child. The adult also used conversation to draw out key ideas, explain, plan and discuss issues and ensure safety and protect the child from harm.

In this example, and many, many others, peer interaction is crucial in the development of science through play. Riley and Savage (1994: 141) state that: 'If children choose an activity and discuss it with their peers, in the course of their conversation the opportunities for play can become a powerful learning opportunity.'

For example, two children in a nursery class decide they are going to play at being explorers, one of them having just read a book about exploring with his mother at home. They dress up in hats and coats and gather maps and magnifying glasses to 'look at the world'. They start to discuss food supplies, transport and what they are looking for 'when they get there'. Other children join in. One child suggests that they go to the North Pole like Winnie the Pooh did. The children agree that this is a good idea and start to plan supplies for a polar trip. The teacher asks them what they will see when they get there. 'Polar bears!' 'Penguins!' 'Santa Claus!' 'Eskimos!' and 'Igloos!' the children call out. They start off on their 'dog sled' and as they 'travel' they discuss what they know about the polar environment and the animals and people within it. Some of their knowledge is correct and some not quite so. When the play is finished the teacher gets out a book on Arctic animals and the children look at it with her, discussing and sharing ideas about life in a polar wilderness for humans and animals, habitats, food supplies and survival mechanisms in extreme cold.

4. KEY STAGE 1 SCIENCE

Guidance as to how and what should be taught to develop science at Key Stage 1 is found in the National Curriculum for England (DfEE/QCA, 1999). There are four areas of knowledge, skills and understanding for science at Key Stage 1:

- Scientific enquiry.

- Life processes and living things.

- Materials and their properties.

- Physical processes.

The skills and knowledge for scientific enquiry are taught through the other three areas of study rather than as a separate subject. For example, children will learn methods of and approaches to scientific enquiry into materials and their properties.

Key skills that are developed through the science curriculum are:

- Communication.

- Application of number.

- IT.

- Working with others.

- Improving own learning and performance.

- Problem solving.

The opportunity for development of these key skills is embedded in the activities children do in science at Key Stage 1. However, it is important to recognize and promote this development through supporting children to use their skills in science and to work independently and as part of a team.

A chance to think

Developing key skills is important in children's general development and their ability to progress onto more complex investigations and experiments and levels of understanding. However, progress with the development of key skills can vary widely between different children.

Exercise 5.5

Observe two children in a class science activity, and using the list above try and assess the skill development that is taking place during the activity for each child. For each child consider:
  How well their skills are developed.
  Which skills are most evident within this activity.
  What could be done to further support the development of skills.
  And also:
  How the skills levels differ between the two children.
  What differences are there in the type and level of support required for each child?

The role of science in the primary curriculum is often seen as having several layers. These include helping children to develop enquiry skills; understanding about the wider meaning of science (becoming literate in science); and making small investigations and understanding basic ideas on which more complex scientific understanding can be based.

Holland and Rowan (1996: 1) suggest that at Key Stage 1: 'By channelling the children's natural curiosity into scientific investigation we can help them to acquire strategies to develop more formal and complex concepts.' Siraj-Blatchford and MacLeod Brudenell suggest that children should be both introduced to key ideas in science and also develop their own investigative skills. They describe this as 'playing the scientist game'.

> The central task of a science education is therefore to give children an appreciation of the historical accomplishments of the scientific community and an introduction to the scientific practices that provide the means by which they are achieved.
>
> (Holland and Rowan, 1999: 6)

They also argue that the key skill within the 'scientist game' is that of reasoning, and that this is developed through scientific enquiry based on experiments and accurate measuring.

Harlen (2000: 13) states that:

> The role of primary science is, therefore, to build a foundation of small ideas that help children understand things in their immediate environment but, most importantly, at the same time to begin to make links between different experience and ideas to build bigger ideas.

4.1 Scientific enquiry

Children are laying down the basic skills for scientific enquiry at Key Stage 1 as well as learning about specific aspects of the world around them. To some extent, the development of enquiry skills is the key issue in Key Stage 1 Science, laying the foundations for more structured investigations at Key Stage 3 and 4, and setting the children on the 'road to discovery' (Wynn and Wiggins, 1997). Scientific enquiry can be achieved through different methods of testing ideas and beliefs about aspects of the environment in which we live. Newton (2000) suggests that the following features are common to most types of scientific enquiry. The process is not linear, but can be repeated again and again as knowledge is increased and refined:

- Something is noticed or observed.
- A tentative hypothesis (explanation) is created to explain what is observed.
- The hypothesis is used to make a prediction about the event.
- An experiment is carried out to test the prediction.
- A conclusion is reached as to whether or not the hypothesis is valid.
- If not, then a retest is carried out to check a revised hypothesis.

(Newton, 2000: 33)

For example, the children may **observe** that plants that do not get water may die. They may form the **hypothesis** that plants need water to live. They may **predict** that if they do not water the plants in the classroom they will wilt and die. They can **experiment** by growing or buying some plants and then depriving them of water and observing the outcome over a period of time. They may **conclude** that some plants do die quite quickly without water, but that others seem to survive longer. They may **revise their hypothesis** to say that some plants need more water to live than others and **retest** by experimenting with the watering needs of different types of plants.

The children could then go on to look at the other needs of plants, warm or cool conditions, light or shade, and make further experiments to confirm that plants have common needs which vary considerably between varieties of plant. In this experiment, it is important to make sure that some variables are kept constant to ensure they do not affect the outcomes of the experiment. These could include warmth, light and air flow. Changes in any of these conditions may also impact on the survival of the plants and therefore must be kept the same for all the plants in order to ensure that we can safely conclude that it is water deprivation that is making the plants die, not something else.

Newton (2000: 43) suggests that exploration is a key skill in scientific enquiry. Exploration is about noticing and observing and describing things and events. Exploration is a skill, which is usually initially developed through activities in the Foundation Stage and the home. This leads to the development of two other types of activity in science:

1. Investigation

- Weighing evidence.
- Comparing evidence with existing ideas.
- Spotting patterns and relationships.
- Explaining what the evidence suggests.
- Drawing some sort of conclusion.

2. Experimentation

- Observing something.
- Coming up with an idea to explain what is observed.
- Predicting what will happen if.
- Designing a fair test to check out the prediction.
- Collecting the evidence.
- Comparing evidence with the original idea.
- Where to from here?

These different approaches will be applied to the other areas of study in Key Stage 1 Science in order to promote pupils' skills in scientific enquiry. However, it is important to remember (with reference to safety issues discussed above) that it is not possible or desirable for children to investigate every scientific aspect of their world through practical activities.

4.2 Life processes and living things

Children will study humans, animals and plants in the local environment in order to cover this part of the National Curriculum. Within this area of study children may explore their own bodies, how they grow, what they can do and the differences between themselves and others. They will learn to identify the factors that differentiate living things from things that have never been alive. They will learn about the different parts of the body, healthy living and what humans, animals and plants need for life.

Newton (2000: 51) lists the seven indicators of life, the presence of all of which differentiates living from non-living things:

- maturation (growth and change)
- locomotion (movement)
- nutrition (feeding)
- respiration (breathing)
- excretion (waste elimination)
- irritability (sensitivity to environment)
- reproduction (producing offspring).

These criteria apply to all living things – humans, animals and plants. Children do not have an instant understanding of the difference between living and non-living things. This develops gradually over time and through experience. Some non-living things fulfil some of these criteria and this can cause confusion. For example, cars and buses, wind and rain all move. It takes time for children to understand the different processes of life, and studies show that it is easier for children to understand growth and movement at an earlier age, and the more complex aspects of life later.

As part of the curriculum for science at Key Stage 1, children may be asked to bring in photos of themselves at a younger age, or as a baby. At the age of 5, Laura was asked to bring a baby photo into class to be put up as part of a display which was being prepared to help the children start to understand the process of maturation. Laura did not mention this project at home until the day it was due, and then she tearfully refused to go to school. As an adopted child, she and her family had no photos of her as a baby, because none had been taken. A photo of Laura at two was substituted and calm restored.

However, this incident reminds us that children do not all have rosy pasts and happy beginnings. Even children as young as 4 and 5 may have complex and difficult histories, reflecting failures in parenting or family breakdown, abuse, loss and separation. Children can feel acutely sensitive about being 'different' and therefore it is important to be aware of the possibility that any activity that delves into family life may be painful for some children. Teachers and teaching assistants need to be aware of the possible sensitive issues and have contingency plans if the activity may cause problems for some children. However, learning about humans is an important part of helping children to develop positive attitudes and values to each other, across cultural, religious and linguistic differences.

4.3   Materials and their properties

Materials are the substances from which our physical environment is structured. They include metals, glass, fibrous materials (polymers), composites (combinations of materials) and alloys (combinations of metals). Children need to know about the range of materials that are in the environment and different ways of classifying these. For example, we can classify a house brick as manufactured (not naturally occurring), a composite (made of several other materials), a solid (not liquid). We can also look at the substances that are used to make a brick and the processes involved, including the application of heat. Is this reversible? Are the substances in different states before they are combined to become a brick e.g. liquid or gas? Why are these particular materials chosen for building houses?

There are any number of materials that can be investigated in this way, by exploring their properties and classifying them according to those properties. Children need to recognize the link between the properties of materials and their uses. For example, bricks are used for building houses because the application of heat makes the combination of materials used hard and strong and this is irreversible. Bricks do not absorb much liquid, they do not dissolve and they will not revert to a liquid state.

Young children may have lots of information about materials from their day-to-day experiences of life at home and in the wider world. This information needs to be extended on and clarified. Cooking is an excellent example of exploring materials and their properties. Combining ingredients such as flour, fat and water can make another material – dough. By applying heat to this dough we can make another material – pastry. Children are often very unclear as to whether materials are manufactured or natural. They may simply not know where flour comes from or how it is processed. Discussing the origins of different materials can help children make sense of the links between different types of materials and to start to classify them as natural or manufactured.

Exploring materials using the senses is central to the activities within this part of the curriculum. Children can explore materials through:

- Sight – what does it look like?

- Smell – what does it smell like?

- Touch – what does it feel like?

- Hearing – what does it sound like?

- Taste – what does it taste like?

It is very important to help young children to recognize that not all materials can safely be explored through all the senses, and that safety warnings must be clear and repeated. Safety issues are discussed in more detail above.

4.4   Physical processes

This part of the Key Stage 1 Science curriculum is concerned with forces – push, pull and twist. Forces that are part of our everyday life include gravity, magnetism, muscular forces, mechanical propulsion, friction and electricity. At Key Stage 1, pupils learn mainly about the properties of electricity, through experiments with batteries, circuits and circuit breakers.

4.5 The role of the teaching assistant

Much of this role is discussed in the section above on the 'The role of the adult'. However, there are some specific areas where teaching assistants can support the learning and teaching of Key Stage 1 Science when working with groups and individual children. These can include finding out what children know about the topic already, clarifying the task and breaking it down into small steps. You may also help children formulate questions to be answered within the task and help them to predict what might happen. Supporting children in carrying out practical activities and maintaining and promoting safe behaviour and use of equipment are also key tasks for the teaching assistant.

It is important to help children to relate the task to the wider world, and ask, 'Why is this relevant to our lives?' This may include linking the activity in with other work the children are doing in other subjects or topics. Teaching assistants can provide a focus (often through questioning) through which children can draw conclusions about the outcomes of the activity. When working with children with different levels of ability, you can support individuals and groups by differentiating more complex tasks for some children. Finally, feeding back to teachers on the success of the activity and any confusions or gaps in knowledge identified can be a great help in the planning process.

There are other more general roles and responsibilities which teaching assistants may have in relation to the management of teaching and learning science. These may include supporting the teacher in planning how to organize the classroom for science activities, helping with displays of materials or children's work, and preparing, storing and maintaining equipment and materials. Teaching assistants also have a role in supporting the teacher to take groups out for trips, nature walks or other explorations of the environment. Supporting the use of IT in science, either through use of software to extend knowledge and understanding or through supporting children in information retrieval is another way in which you may work with children in Key Stage 1 science.

4.6 IT in science

This area of responsibility really needs a special mention. The uses of IT in the classroom are multiplying steadily, with increased access to both hardware and software and increased expertise among both staff and pupils. Harlen (2000: 100) identifies several areas where IT can be used to support science in the primary classroom:

- Word-processing – recording the activity and outcomes.

- Data-logging – recording information sent directly to the computer through probes connected to the computer using suitable software.

- Data-handling – software can create line graphs, pie charts or bar charts from information entered manually or through the probes mentioned above.

- Simulations and modelling – for simulating processes which are not accessible or too dangerous to do in reality.

- Spreadsheets and databases – to organize information which has been collected so that patterns can become apparent.

- Internet – for research and resources.

- CD-ROMs – for information.

It is very possible that at present only some of these applications will be available in your workplace. However, this is an area of rapid development and new applications are being developed for schools and adopted by schools all the time. The uses of IT with children in a particular school will be dictated by the age and experience of the children, the extent of the resources of the school, and the expertise among staff in using and developing IT as a tool for learning and teaching. However, in science activities children's learning can be enhanced and supported through the range of information they can access, the sense of being linked to a wider scientific community and the potential for recording and assessing data in a variety of ways.

CONCLUSION

Supporting Key Stage 1 Science can be a very rewarding part of a teaching assistant's role. In this subject, children can draw on a range of skills and abilities – literacy, numeracy, IT skills and their own creativity to explore and make sense of the world around them. At the very least, sharing in these explorations can be great fun! But, children are also making important discoveries about their world and the objects and living things within it. Providing them with a safe and structured environment in which to do this is crucial, and you have a major role in making sure this is achieved. Children need to understand the ways in which scientific exploration is conducted and how we find out about the characteristics and properties of different materials or aspects of our world. It is important for you to be aware of and to convey to the children that science takes place as part of an ongoing process, and in the light of an existing body of scientific knowledge. Finding out more about science in the present and the past is an essential part of developing this awareness.

NOTES FOR FURTHER READING

Bloomfield, P., de Boo, M. and Rawlings, B. (2000)
'Exploring our world'. Chapter 17 in Drury, L., Campbell, R. and Miller, I. (eds)
Looking at Early Years Education and Care.
London: David Fulton.

Brown, G. and Wragg, E. (1993)
Questioning.
London: Routledge.

DfEE/QCA (1999)
National Curriculum for England.
www.nc.uk.net
Sudbury: QCA.

Harlen, W. (2000)
The Teaching of Science in Primary Schools, third edn.
London: David Fulton.

Holland, C. and Rowan, J. (1996)
The Really Practical Guide to Primary Science, second edn.
Cheltenham: Stanley Thornes.

Newton, L. (2000)
Meeting the Standards in Primary Science – a Guide to the ITT NC.
London: RoutledgeFalmer.

O'Hara, M. (2000)
Teaching 3–8.
London: Continuum.

Qualifications and Curriculum Authority (QCA) (2000)
Curriculum Guidance for the Foundation Stage.
Sudbury: QCA.

Riley, J. and Savage, J. (1994)
'Bulbs, buzzers and batteries – play and science', Chapter 11 in Moyles, J. (ed.) *The Excellence of Play.*
Milton Keynes: Open University Press.

Siraj-Blatchford, J. and MacLeod Brudenell, I. (1999)
Supporting Science, Design and Technology in the Early Years.
Milton Keynes: Open University Press.

Wynn, C. M. and Wiggins, A. C. (1997)
The Five Biggest Ideas in Science.
New York: John Wiley and Sons, Inc.

CHAPTER 6

Assessment and Recording

Teaching assistants have a significant role to play in the monitoring and assessment of groups of children and individual children whom they are involved in supporting. Assessment is a more major part of the activities in primary classrooms, more so since the introduction of the National Curriculum and the Early Learning Goals formalized the curriculum for young children. The role of assessment in monitoring the performance of individual children, whole schools and the broader education system has been well established over the last few years.

But what is assessment for? O'Hara (2000: 102) states that assessment is to ensure that teachers know:

- What children know.
- What they can do.
- Where they need to go next.

Assessment provides the basis on which the next round of planning for teaching and learning can take place. If assessment is ongoing and accurate, teachers can plan teaching and learning from a baseline of knowledge as to where the children have already progressed.

Assessment is not a single process, nor does it all take place formally or at preset stages in the school year. Formal assessment has a role to play, but is only one part of the wide range of assessment processes which take place throughout each school year and the whole of Key Stage 1. Children are formally assessed at the end of Key Stage 1 through Standard Assessment Tasks (SATs), which measure children's progress against a nationally determined range of criteria across particular parts of the curriculum. SATs results give the teacher feedback on the child's progress and abilities. They also give the school feedback on the whole class achievement, which can be compared with previous classes at the end of Key Stage 1, and compared with other schools' results within the LEA, and nationwide. Each school will have set targets for achievement and the SATs results will be judged against these targets. SATs are also used to prepare the LEA's 'league tables' which are published in the local press and which show how different schools have performed within the LEA.

But SATs are only a small part of the assessment process in schools. Although they have a high profile because they are nationally determined and the results are published, they rarely tell teachers and schools much they do not already know about the children in their care. While SATs can be typified as 'summative' assessment – assessment that takes place at the end of a phase of the curriculum –

schools are also involved in ongoing, formal and informal 'formative' assessment. This type of assessment is the day-to-day monitoring and judging of children's work, which informs teachers of the ongoing progress of individuals and the whole class.

All assessment is vitally important in the teaching and learning process because:

- It gives feedback to teachers on the effectiveness of learning and teaching strategies.

- It helps teachers become aware of areas that the whole class needs to work on more or in a different way.

- It helps teachers to recognize specific problems or areas of lack of progress a particular child may have.

- It helps teachers to assess the rate of progress the class and individual children are making.

- It is the basis of feedback to children as a group or individuals and provides material for giving praise and acknowledging progress.

- It provides information which can be shared with parents.

- It can help teachers and heads to become aware of deficits in resources, both human and physical.

- It helps teachers judge their own performance and planning and make adjustments as required.

All assessment is based on the process of judging children's progress and achievements against known criteria. When SATs are taken at the end of Key Stage 1, this is a more formal process based on clearly stated criteria. However, during the more informal processes of assessment, the criteria are not necessarily so clearly stated and the assessment is not usually achieved through tests. So more informal assessment could include:

- A teacher noting that a child's writing development is well advanced compared to the rest of the class.

- A teaching assistant reporting verbally to the teacher that a group she had been working with found the set activity confusing and too hard.

- A parent volunteer commenting to the teacher that a child who had some behavioural problems in school worked quietly and with concentration during drawing and painting activities.

- A teaching assistant working with an individual child reports that the child has become unhappy about leaving the class to do one-to-one work during parts of her literacy work.

A chance to think

One of the key purposes of assessment is to inform the teacher and the school as a whole of the effectiveness of teaching and learning activities, and the levels of support for individual children. Teachers make constant adjustments to their planned activities in response to the feedback they get based on assessments of individual children, groups and the whole class. This is a crucial part of the teaching and learning cycle, promoting responsiveness to children's real needs and ensuring that these needs are met at the level of the individual child, small groups and the whole class.

Exercise 6.1

Look at the examples of informal assessment above, and for each one, decide what should be done in response to this information. Compare your answers with the sample answers on page 166.

Good standards of assessment are based on effective monitoring and recording systems which ensure there is a written record of the assessment outcomes. The process of recording, how this is planned and implemented, what is recorded and the conclusions drawn are an important part of the assessment process, ensuring that assessment is ongoing, accurate and informative. Assessment, which is not based on accurate and ongoing recording, may be ineffective or inaccurate.

Monitoring is the ongoing process by which particular areas of development are observed and noted to ensure progress is being made as expected, or to highlight any problems or delays. Monitoring can be about specific issues relating to particular children or more general ones. Much of it is based on good observation skills and a shared approach between staff.

1. TYPES OF ASSESSMENT

A number of different types of assessments are used with young children. It is important to note that the choice of type of assessment is not random. We choose the type depending on what we want to assess and for what purpose. The type of assessment used must match the outcomes required if it is to be effective. This does not mean that there are no choices to be made. Very often there will be different ways in which a particular assessment can be made. Choices may depend on the resources available and the forms of assessment that are most familiar and seem most effective to those involved. In some circumstances, it is helpful to draw information for assessment purposes from more than one source, to strengthen the judgements that may then take place.

Choices of assessment must also be geared to the needs of young children and the possible impact of different assessment methods on their confidence and progress. There have been some criticisms of formal testing of 7-year-olds because of the possible negative impact of this type of assessment on some young children's self-esteem and confidence. The type of assessment used must therefore both fit the purpose of the assessment process and meet the needs of the children involved. While some types of assessment are so 'feather light' the children are more or less unaware of them, others are more obvious and therefore have more impact.

1.1 Summative assessment

As discussed above, summative assessments take place at the end of a specific phase of learning. Summative assessment, such as the SATs described above, sum up what the child has achieved at a specific time or stage of learning. Plans are in hand to introduce this type of assessment for children moving from the Foundation Stage to Key Stage 1, as well as children moving between Key Stages. Summative assessment usually also takes place at the end of each school year, providing a basis for teachers to feedback to parents on their children's progress within the school year. This end-of-year assessment can also be used to inform the teacher of the next class up, in terms of his or her planning. It can be used to determine if special educational needs (SEN) are evident in respect of individual children, and what sort of support is required to assist the child to make progress. Not all summative assessment is based on a formal process. End-of-year assessment is often based on both informal and formal formative assessments that have taken place over a period of time.

Summative assessment is important in checking each child's progress against expected levels of attainment (criteria), but has less use in helping teachers plan their teaching and learning or give regular feedback to children and their parents, because it only takes place periodically.

1.2 Formative assessment

Formative assessment is more ongoing, whether it is based on formal methods or informal methods. It is the constant feedback teachers use to decide what sort of teaching and learning, support and encouragement their pupils need, either as individuals or as part of the whole class. This feedback comes from a wide range of informal sources:

- Daily examination of children's work.
- Feedback from reading records.
- The answers children give to questions.
- The questions children ask.
- The mistakes children are making and the problems children are encountering with specific activities.
- Comments and concerns of parents.
- Comments and concerns of the children.

More formal sources include assessment that is planned beforehand such as:

- Tests e.g. spelling tests, maths tests.
- Criteria-based assessment (assessing children during tasks against a pre-set lists of criteria).

- Homework.

Formative assessment comes from a wide range of sources of information which are collated and seen as a whole by the class teacher. This type of assessment draws on the skills of all staff and volunteers in the classroom and the wider school, on the views and observations of parents and children, and on the expertise of specialist staff from outside the school. Formative assessment can help to diagnose particular difficulties children may have, as well as provide an ongoing record of the children's progress.

For example, Kerry, 6, had problems with her handwriting to the point where she actively avoided writing tasks and sometimes refused to write. In discussion with her parents, it became clear that they were concerned about aspects of Kerry's physical co-ordination as well as her performance at school. Kerry's parents arranged paediatric assessment for Kerry through the local children's hospital. The physiotherapist found that Kerry had poor strength and stability in her shoulders and upper body, which made writing a difficult task for her. In consultation with the teacher and the Special Educational Needs Co-ordinator (SENCO) and the direct involvement of two support workers, Kerry was supported with a programme of physiotherapy at home and at school in order to help her gain strength and stability in her upper body, and ultimately to help her make progress with her handwriting. She also received extra help in class and was encouraged to use the computer to develop literacy skills so that her writing delays had less general impact on her literacy development.

1.3 Approaches to assessment

There are a number of different measures against which a child's work can be judged, and it is important to know which is being used and why. They are:

- National criteria such as the National Curriculum level descriptors, which set general attainment standards against which work can be measured.

- The average of the class, which may not reflect the above, but which can give information about the child's level of development in relation to the rest of the group.

- The child's own progress rates in terms of her individual development.

Clearly, SATs fall into the first category, so inevitably children will be assessed against national criteria at the end of Key Stage 1. Assessing children in relation to the norm for the rest of the class is useful for a number of reasons:

- Having an understanding of the range of levels of ability within the class to inform planning.

- Identifying children who need extra support.

- Identifying when tasks need to be differentiated to meet the needs of all children.

- Feedback to parents.

- Children's individual progress.

Judging a child's progress against his previous achievements is a sound basis for giving praise and encouragement and helping unconfident children to recognize that they have progressed. Children with SEN have this process formalized through their Individual Education Plans (IEPs) which set targets for the child to progress towards. There targets reviewed on a regular basis. This helps the child, parents, teachers and support workers to recognize and praise areas where progress is being made, and review support in areas where progress is less evident.

Effective assessment is usually based on a range of different approaches to provide the assessors with a full picture of the child's abilities. One type of assessment may simply not give enough information or may not provide all we need to know about the child's ability to learn and progress to date. For example, when Dan was 6, his delays in learning to read and write seemed to dominate the view of his learning progress held by his parents, school and, sadly, himself. With the support of other types of assessment, however, Dan's oral skills became a much stronger focus for assessment giving a broader and more encouraging picture of his progress and ability to learn. Dan's self-confidence and self-esteem benefited directly from this wider view of his abilities and this more positive view of self was reflected in his learning.

Using different approaches also means that different individuals involved in the child's learning can contribute to the assessment process. Different assessment methods may be effective with different children depending on a number of factors:

- Gender.

- Culture and language.

- Particular skills and strengths.

- Response to different assessment methods.

Assessing to determine children's strengths as well as their areas for further development is an important basis for positive and encouraging feedback to both parents and children.

A chance to think

Assessing children in different ways to gain a full picture of their abilities is dependent to a large degree on knowing the child's characteristics, levels of confidence and areas of interest. If we consistently use assessment tools that favour one type of child rather than another, this may have a long-term impact on their confidence. For example, when IQ tests were first used, many argued that they measured the sorts of abilities that were most likely to be found in white, middle-class children. These children did do better in the tests in general, and this was sometimes used to support the notion that they were more intelligent. However, others argue that the tests only assessed certain types of intelligence, which did not reflect the range of skills and abilities of all types of children.

Exercise 6.2

Think about some of the children you work with and the ways in which their work is assessed. For one or two children, answer the following questions:

1. What sort of assessment best demonstrates this child's range of ability?

2. What type of assessment does not seem to best reflect the child's knowledge, skills and understanding?

3. Are there any explanations you can give for this, based on your knowledge of the individual children?

Share your ideas with the teacher or a mentor.

1.4   Skills and methods for assessment

Assessment can be achieved through a number of different approaches, and using particular skills. These include:

- Observation.

- Questions and answers.

- Listening to oral work, discussions or conversations.

- Assessing products (children's work such as written work, drawings and constructions).

Observation is a tool for assessment that is used regularly in the Foundation Stage, but is perhaps less emphasized at Key Stage 1. However, in practice much informal formative assessment is based on day-to-day observations of children's work, behaviour and verbal contributions. Observations can be conducted formally, where specific aspects of a child or children's work or behaviour are focused on and recorded, often against pre-set criteria; or it can be informal, in the sense that adults working with children will be observing their activities and behaviour all the time. Observations can be timed or can accord with a framework of issues that are to be recorded (Jarvis and Lamb, 2000).

Skills for observing children include:

- Noting behaviour and speech.

- Being clear about what aspect of the child's learning or behaviour is being observed.

- Being objective in the assessment of what is observed.

- Spending time and being patient.

Objectivity is important. It is all too easy to have a set view of what we expect to observe about a particular child and then to 'see' only those behaviours that reinforce this view. Although those behaviours may be evident, there may be other behaviours that give a different view of the child's ability or understanding. Using questions and answers to judge the extent of a child's understanding is an important tool for assessment. Questions and answers help us to assess the processes underpinning the child's apparent understanding, and ensure that the child knows how he reached the 'right' answer. Although it is positive for children to work together in pairs and groups, question and answer can help to ascertain if all children in the group have fully understood the task or activity, or whether one or two children have led the group. Question and answer can also help children in their thought processes. By thinking questions through and formulating and articulating answers, children can consolidate and integrate new learning. However, question and answer can be difficult for shy children or those who lack confidence or who are worried about being 'wrong'. Skills for question and answer include:

- Asking open questions (questions that demand a sentence or more for the answer).

- Avoiding closed questions (questions that can only be answered by 'yes' or 'no').

- Formulating clear simple questions that are not ambiguous and do not have several parts to them.

- Being patient, waiting for an answer.

- Being sensitive to children's fear of failure.

- Avoiding a barrage of questions that may seem like an interrogation.

Question and answer is a two-way process. By encouraging children to ask questions themselves, we can learn a lot about the gaps in children's knowledge and understanding.

In many ways, listening is an integral part of both observation and question and answer, but because of the crucial role it plays in assessing young children's knowledge and understanding, listening deserves a particular mention. Active listening is a key skill for anyone working with young children, across the range of roles and responsibilities within the school. Active listening involves not only using our senses to hear what children are saying, but also creating the conditions in which communication can take place and ensuring that children are encouraged to communicate effectively. Adult behaviours that encourage active listening include:

- Making time and space to listen.

- Using non-verbal communication to encourage the child to speak e.g. eye contact, smiles, positive body language.

- Being patient and giving the child time to speak.

- Listening for feelings or areas of uncertainty behind the speech.

- Listening to what is not said.

Behaviours that can discourage children from communicating verbally include:

- Finishing sentences for the child.

- Assuming you know what is to be said before the child has finished speaking.

- Telling the child what you think too early in the sequence.

- Interrupting, hurrying the child up or moving on without listening.

- Not making time, space or effort to listen.

- Showing impatience or the desire to move on through non-verbal communication e.g. being poised to move on or looking away.

By listening carefully to children's explanations, the types of questions they ask and the sorts of concerns they have, you can assess their areas of understanding and knowledge and areas of uncertainty or confusion with a great deal of accuracy. Active listening can be time consuming and usually works best either in one-to-one situations or small groups.

Assessing the actual products of children's work, such as written work, records of investigations, drawings, paintings, models and constructions is an important method of tracking progress. These items remain as a physical record of a child's individual learning development, which can be tracked over time and shared with parents. They are a useful basis for discussion about progress with the child, for praise and encouragement and and to act plans and targets for the future. O'Hara (2000: 113) comments: 'Concrete outcomes assessed in conjunction with teacher–pupil discussions can be very helpful in enabling children to become more involved and take an active part in the process of assessment.' Concrete examples of children's work can also be compared across the class to determine the overall level and to inform future planning.

1.5 Assessment through play

One other important opportunity for assessment that has not been discussed so far is observing and discussing children's play. Assessment through play has a significant role in the Foundation Stage, where children are assessed more holistically rather than in separate areas of development or subjects. However, assessment through play is probably less common at Key Stage 1, although it has much value. Perhaps this is partly due to some of the difficulties that can be encountered when planning to assess through play, and partly due to the reduction in time for play at Key Stage 1. Wood and Attfield (1996: 123) suggest the following problems might arise when considering assessment through play:

- It may not be taken seriously by those who do not value learning through play.

- Play does not always predict behaviour later in life.

- 'Deep and serious' play may not fit well in schools.

- Some play is less valued by adults in terms of its educational content.

Play can also be unpredictable, making planning for assessment difficult to implement at times. However, despite this, play offers unprecedented opportunities for assessing many aspects of children's learning and development. In Bennett *et al.'s* (1997: 84) study of teaching through play, they quote one of their case study teacher's comments 'that play offered opportunities for gaining a "much better picture of the whole child's intellectual, emotional and social development" and "the sum total of their experience to date".'

She went on to state that she 'was able to assess the National Curriculum subjects through play activities because of the "exploratory, investigative emphasis" in maths and science, and by incorporating "a strong emphasis on literacy through play".'

Clearly assessment through play is a useful tool, which could be developed further within the context of Key Stage 1. Skills for assessing play include:

- Good observation skills.

- Good listening skills.

- An understanding of the interconnected nature of the child's different areas of development.

- A clear understanding of the role of play in development (see Chapter 2).

Assessment through play can support the development of understanding about the following issues influencing learning and teaching in the class:

- The nature of group interactions.

- The social skills of individual children.

- The emotional factors influencing learning.

- The ways in which different areas of learning have been integrated and linked to each other.

- The ways in which children can support each other's learning.

Assessment of children with SEN at play can give relevant insights into the range of developmental delays or emotional and social problems that may be influencing the child's learning progress. These insights can inform not only the content of the support the child receives, but also how the support is delivered. For example, a child who plays well with peers and has good social skills may benefit from being supported in a small group. A child who has limited social skills may benefit from peer mentoring or a 'circle of friends'.

Sayeed and Guerin (2000: 49) suggests a model of Play Based Assessment (PBA) for children with SEN, which uses the familiar medium of play to assess the child's learning patterns. An observational schedule addressing specific aspects of the child's development to be assessed can be drawn up as a recording tool. This type of assessment can provide a range of insights into the strengths and areas for development of a child with SEN, and can be shared between home and school.

The opportunities available to assess through play are more limited at Key Stage 1, but should be incorporated in the range of assessment tools available to broaden and clarify other assessment outcomes. For example, if we wish to know if children can apply maths principles they have learned in the numeracy hour, we may encourage and support them to play 'shops and shopping'. Do the children use maths in 'real' situations? Can they apply their learning? Have all the children understood the principles? These are important questions in terms of curriculum planning and feedback on the value of previous activities.

Discussion and conversation about the content of play is an important part of assessment through play, providing the assessor with an understanding of the child's knowledge and skills, feelings and levels of independence.

1.6 Feedback

Giving feedback is a crucial element in the assessment process. It is not much use to children to be assessed if the outcomes of that assessment cannot or are not translated into information that will support and encourage the child's learning in the future.

Feedback comes in many forms, formal and informal, written and verbal, instant and delayed. Some feedback is associated with summative assessment, for example, annual reports and discussions at end-of-year parents' evenings, and SATs results. Some is associated with formative assessment, and can include feedback on written work or oral work, groupwork and individual work, projects and play. It can include written comments and verbal comments, grades and marks out of a total, for example, spelling test results. Feedback appears as comments in a child's reading record, ticks and comments on written numeracy work, praise for the whole class or a particular group, a child being asked to show work to the class or even to the whole school. Feedback can come in the form of stickers ('Star of the Week'), certificates ('Super Speller') or comments to parents at home time.

Whatever the form feedback takes, it should always be based on the following principles:

- Feedback should be positive as well as negative.

- It should be considered and pertinent to the particular achievement.

- It should link that achievement to the child's overall progress where possible.

- It should suggest areas for further development where appropriate.

- It should not be critical, overly negative or condemning.

- It should involve the child's views and opinions which should be actively sought.

- It should be shared with others where appropriate.

- It should never damage a child's self-esteem or confidence.

- Praise should be genuine and based on progress.

Feedback is often given at a high level in primary schools, based on the principle of supporting self-esteem and good levels of self-confidence. Children need to know they are doing well and progress is being made. They will benefit from being in an environment where praise and encouragement are the norm. However, there are a few pitfalls, which need to be considered alongside this positive approach. Children will not necessarily benefit from the 'that's nice, just pop it over there' syndrome, which can be found in some establishments. If children learn that standard praise comments will be issued for every piece of work they do, this may not promote high standards. Work needs to be properly examined and discussed, and the child's view on its quality sought, in order to give genuine and valuable feedback. Feedback has more meaning when it is focused on a few pieces of work or aspects of progress rather than being general. Over-use of praise can devalue it in the children's eyes, so although praise is very important, children should feel it is based on real progress or achievement. For example, Damien, 7, was so used to 'smiley faces' on his work, to encourage his slow progress, that he drew them on his work himself before completing it. Any value they had as form of positive feedback had faded by this stage, and new methods of giving Damien praise had to be sought. Giving feedback that is carefully considered, immediate and based on a considered assessment of the child's work, however, can be a vital part of the learning process and central to the child's overall development.

2. RECORDING

We may be forgiven for believing that we currently live in a society where if something is not recorded, it does not exist! The emphasis on written records has increased greatly in recent years, mainly in response to a growth in the range of areas over which schools must show accountability and an increased level of requirement to report outcomes and progress to parents, governors, the Local Education Authority (LEA) and the DfES.

Many teachers feel that they spend a vast amount of time on paperwork, and this impacts on all aspects of school life and everyone who works within a school. Certainly, all teaching assistants, whatever their individual roles and responsibilities, will almost inevitably be involved in some form of recording. This could be in connection with the progress of individual pupils, it could be related to targets for children with IEPs or it could be recording the outcomes of a single activity involving a group of children.

All recording is related to assessment of progress and achievement. Some recording, such as reading records, tick lists relating to particular activities and daily records made in respect of some children, are part of formative assessment, contributing to an ongoing cycle of planning in the classroom. Other recording is summative, such as children's annual reports, SATs results and review reports for children with SEN. However, whatever the purpose of recording there are a number of issues that need to be considered in order to record effectively. These include:

- The purposes of the recording.

- The format of the record.

- How the information will be used.

- Who is it going to be shared with.

- Whether it is confidential.

- Where it will be stored.

The purposes of recording are many and varied. It is important to consider why you are recording on a particular occasion, because the process will be different for different purposes. For example, a child's reading record will contain information about the child's progress with reading and the books he/she has read. However, where a child has an IEP, there may be more detailed records required to chart the child's progress towards meeting a particular target. For example, there may be a timesheet to show how long the child has been able to work independently, or write her name or read certain words. If we do not consider the purposes of recording, the records may not contain the information needed, or they may contain too much information.

The format of a record can vary widely, depending on the purposes of the record. The formats commonly used in school include written records, tick lists, compilations of students' work, observation notes and annual reports. Children's workbooks, containing comments and marking results are a record in their own right. The format chosen will depend on the purpose of the record, the time available to make the record and the depth of information required. For example, a tick list does not give information about the level or quality of an achievement, only that it has been achieved. Written records give more detail and can contain evaluations of the quality and level of the work. They can provide an important basis for discussion with the child, the parent or professionals from other agencies. They can be used to recommend new approaches, targets and areas to work on as well as to assess work, give positive feedback and comment on progress.

The purposes of the information will also determine the nature of the record. Is it a quick note to the teacher to tell them that a child is struggling with subtraction? Or is it a more detailed reading record to help parents know what to read with their child at home? The tone, language and content may vary according to the uses the information will be put to. A report to the review meeting for a child with SEN may be written in more formal language than a note to the teacher.

All recorded information is shared with others, and this may also influence how the information is recorded, the type of language used and the detail involved. It is important to consider who will see this record, how they will use the information in it, and whether the information is adequate and appropriate for the uses others have for it. Every record, whatever the purpose and whoever it is intended for should be written objectively and fairly, without negative comment on the child as an individual. For example, there is a real difference between writing, 'Shabana was naughty all morning and refused to do her work' and 'Shabana had difficulty concentrating and staying on task this morning. She walked around the room several times and tried to look at other children's work. She did not sit down when asked to.' The first tells other people very little about Shabana's behaviour, but it does label her as 'naughty'. The second tells us what Shabana actually did, giving a starting point for areas to work on with her. A good 'rule of thumb' when writing anything about a child is to assume that both the parents and the child could read the record and not to include anything that you would not like them to read. This does not mean that you should not record difficult or problematic behaviour, just that you should record it objectively, describing the behaviour not the child.

Confidentiality issues will be dealt with in more detail in Chapter 8. However, when recording it is important to know who you are expected to share the information with and to restrict discussion of it to those individuals. Obviously, the teacher will have access to any recording you do, possibly the SENCO, other teaching staff or the head and possibly workers from other agencies, through SEN reviews and other meetings. Parents may have direct access to your records, or your information may contribute to teacher's records, which are then shared with parents. Most information is not highly confidential, but it is important to be aware that children can be very sensitive about any perceived delays or problems in their achievement. Confidentiality is as much about supporting the child and respecting his/her feelings as it is about meeting adult requirements. If in doubt, check with the teacher regarding who should have access to records or with whom they can be discussed. Some records may be much more sensitive. For example, each child in public care (child 'looked after' by the Local Authority) will have a Personal Education Plan (PEP) to support his or her learning. Some of the information contained in these may relate to problems from the child's earlier life, which should be kept strictly confidential.

The issue of how records are stored relates to confidentiality of information and to access. Records need to be kept in places that are safe, accessible to those who have access rights and inaccessible to those who do not, depending on the level of confidentiality required. The school and the individual teacher have responsibility for ensuring that records are properly stored and your own records should be kept within this system. Avoid leaving records lying around for others to see or read, and make sure that records do not go missing.

A chance to think

Recording, which has to be done, can sometimes feel like an unimportant but tedious part of the day's work. Heavier requirements to keep written records about all aspects of school life and pupil progress can feel overwhelming when you are busy. Recording seems less pointless if the purposes are clear and it makes a real contribution to helping children's progress and achievement.

Exercise 6.3

Think about the different recording you have done this week and answer the following questions for each type:

1. What was the purpose of the record?

2. Did the format of the record fit the purpose?

3. Who was the record for?

4. How were confidentiality issues addressed and who had access to the record?

5. How did the record support the child or children's progress?

If this exercise raises any questions about recording, discuss them with the teacher or a mentor.

---

3. THE TEACHING ASSISTANT'S ROLE

The role of the teaching assistant in assessment and recording will vary considerably depending on the specific work you are each involved in. All assessment and recording activities will be agreed with the teacher and possibly other members of the school staff or other professionals involved with a particular child. The teaching assistant's role is to:

- Make assessments as agreed with the teacher and record these as planned.

- Keep such records as have been agreed in the format and level of depth required.

- Report back to the teacher on the progress of individual children and groups of children as required.

- Identify learning points which will inform future planning e.g. areas of a subject that the child or children needs to do more work on.

- Identify successes, achievements and breakthroughs and share these with the teacher.

- Give feedback to the child as required.

- Report back to any other professionals or parents as agreed.

Much of the assessment and recording you do will contribute to the teacher's formative and summative reports. Some, however, will be the definitive record, particularly where you work directly with one child. The formative assessment you are involved in should contribute to the teacher's planning process and the teaching and learning which takes place in the classroom.

The role of the teaching assistant also includes ensuring records are fair and open, and that they avoid subjective and possibly damaging comments about the child as described above in the example of Shabana. It is very easy to develop a particular view of a child, which may then affect all our dealings with that child, especially if the child has difficult or demanding behaviour patterns. These fixed views or stereotypes can prevent us from seeing the child's progress and achievements clearly, as we tend to observe only the aspects of the child's behaviour that support our fixed view. Stereotyping children can limit the effective support they are given, it can reinforce negative self-esteem and poor self-confidence in the child and it can mean the opportunity to build on areas of strength goes unnoticed.

Finally, it is important to remember that your role is not just as a human recording instrument, passing information on to the teacher. You bring your own skill and expertise, knowledge and understanding to the process, enriching the assessment with your own evaluation and interpretation of what is observed or recorded. This is a very valuable aspect of the teaching assistant's role in assessment and recording and one that should be developed to the full. The sorts of knowledge and understanding which can be usefully brought to bear when evaluating assessment information are:

- How young children learn best.

- Child development and developmental delays.

- Your specific knowledge of individual children's learning needs.

- Your knowledge of the child or children's ongoing progress and achievements.

- Your knowledge and understanding of how best to support children sensitively and effectively.

- Your knowledge and understanding of effective verbal and written communication.

CONCLUSIONS

Teaching assistants have a major role to play in the assessment processes taking place in primary classrooms. Teachers need assessment information for planning and for tracking pupil's progress, yet often the logistics of assessing large classes are highly challenging. Teaching assistants have increasingly supported the assessment

117

process in partnership with the teacher and other staff. Developing confidence in your ability to use assessment processes effectively and to understand the types and purposes of assessment is a key role for teaching assistants. Giving feedback to children, and recording and evaluating assessment information are all tasks that are becoming more a part of that role. As teaching assistants continue to gain prominence in classrooms, this role seems likely to continue to expand, requiring the further development of the range of skills and abilities discussed above.

NOTES FOR FURTHER READING

Bennett, N., Wood, L. and Rogers, S. (1997)
Teaching Through Play – Teacher's Thinking and Classroom Practice.
Milton Keynes: Open University Press.

Jarvis, J. and Lamb, S. (2000)
'Supporting children with communication difficulties'. Chapter 7 in Drury, R., Miller, L. and Campbell, R. (eds) *Looking at Early Years Education and Care.*
London: David Fulton.

O'Hara, M. (2000)
Teaching 3–8.
London: Continuum.

Sayeed, Z. and Guerin, E. (2000)
'Play assessment and culture'. Chapter 4 in Wolfendale, S. (ed.) *Meeting Special Needs in the Early Years.*
London: David Fulton.

Wood, E. and Attfield, J. (1996)
Play, Learning and the Early Childhood Curriculum.
London: Paul Chapman.

CHAPTER 7

Supporting Children's Learning and Behaviour in School

INTRODUCTION

Good standards of behaviour are not just about the actions of individual children or groups of children. Developing good standards of behaviour is part of children's learning, and how effectively this learning takes place depends very much on how behaviour is managed across the whole school.

In this chapter, we will explore the factors that contribute to problems with behaviour across the school, and the ways in which this might affect children's learning. The role of the teaching assistant in contributing to whole school development in this area is discussed. The teaching assistant's responsibilities are discussed in the context of their role within the school and their relationship with the class teacher. Behavioural factors influencing the effectiveness of work with individual children and groups are discussed. The development of a framework of rules and policies within school, which support and promote good standards of behaviour, is discussed. Strategies for dealing with potential and actual conflict are explored, along with limitations on the teaching assistant's role in managing behaviour in school. The various approaches to supporting children in difficulties, dealing with distressed children, and working with children to modify their behaviour are also examined.

A key theme is the development of interpersonal skills for supporting effective behaviour management. These include good communication, responsiveness, developing positive relationships with children and using disciplinary measures appropriately.

1. POLICIES AND RULES

Every school should have a policy on behaviour which clearly outlines the expectations placed on pupils within the school. This policy is drawn up and approved by the governing body, including the headteacher. Parents are usually asked to comment on the policy and contribute to developing it over time. School behaviour policies are important in terms of creating a common standard which can be worked towards by all sectors of the school community. However, like all policies, the value of a behaviour policy can only be measured by the extent to which it is implemented. Put simply, a policy is merely a piece of paper unless action is taken to make sure that the proposals within it are put into practice. Policies on behaviour tend to give an outline of expectations of children's behaviour and when and how disciplinary measures will be taken. These policies are supported by home–school agreements, which are contracts signed by parents and children, stating that they agree to abide by certain rules within school. These include, amongst other things, standards of expected behaviour. Home–school agreements are not compulsory, but are used as a method of stating what the school expects from parents and pupils, and what parents and pupils can expect from the school. Research into home–school agreements, which were introduced in all schools in 1999, has shown, however, that not all schools have found them helpful or influential in improving standards of behaviour (Parker-Jenkins *et al.* 2001). Because they are not compulsory, many do not get signed or returned to school, and the conditions within them are not binding. However, home–school agreements may fulfil an important function in raising the issue of standards and expectations within schools and between schools and parents.

Other policies that support the development of good standards across the whole school include bullying policies, which state not only what should happen if a child is bullied, but also the types of behaviour that could constitute bullying. Often bullying is seen simply as incidents of physical assault. However, for many children who are bullied, their experience includes a much wider range of intimidating behaviour by others. Bullying can include verbal abuse; exclusion from play and other activities; enforced social isolation; threats of violence; racist abuse; being forced to give property or money to others; being forced to obey the directives of others. Bullying policies are important in determining what is perceived as bullying and how the school will respond to incidents. However, promoting a whole school policy on good standards of behaviour is an important part of the process of preventing bullying behaviour from developing in the first place.

Finding a balance between the needs of young children to be supported and feel confident in the school environment, and the need for order and good behaviour is not always easy. Too many rules, too strict an environment, and children may become anxious and unable to act on their own initiative for fear of doing 'something wrong'. Too few rules, too lax an environment, and children's learning may be impaired by the chaos that could ensue. Policies on behaviour tend to emphasize a sensible approach to behaviour in school, based on health and safety requirements and the need for children to learn in an orderly and well-managed environment. Policies often emphasize the need for mutual consideration and respect for others within all sectors of the school, to promote positive social attitudes and beliefs.

Children need to know what is expected of them in order to behave well. Learning school rules can take time and children may be worried about breaking rules because they do not really know what the rules are. For example, when Ben first entered school at the age of four and a half, his play reflected some of his concerns about understanding and following school rules. Every night for the first six weeks of school, he played at 'schools', a game which involved lining up small figures and telling them school rules (and telling them off for not following the rules). Ben was not being told off for not following rules, but clearly he was concerned that this could happen. The play helped Ben absorb the rules and expectations of him in school and as he became more comfortable with these and more confident that he was behaving as expected, the game was gradually abandoned.

For young children just entering school, there is a need to explain rules patiently and repeatedly until they start to understand what is expected. Children may not have had previous experiences of having to be quiet and sit still for the length of time school sometimes demands of them. They may have to learn about turn taking, lining-up and putting their hands up. They may not remember that it is a good idea to go to the toilet at break time. For example, in school assembly early on in the school year, reception class children were sitting at the front of the hall in a long row. The assembly is fairly long, but broken up into different items providing variety and interest. However, some of the youngest children are starting to loll about or fidget after about twenty minutes, leaning on each other and fiddling with their shoelaces, each other's hair and anything else they can find to twiddle. One child is lying down, another is whispering loudly to her neighbour and a third is acting out something taking place in her imagination. The teaching assistant at the end of the row leans forward and quietly reminds them that they should be sitting up, cross-legged and not fiddling. The children are not necessarily being disobedient, but they have forgotten what is expected of them for a short time and need reminding. It is important to note that the teaching assistant was quiet and gentle in her reminder, and her tone of voice, although firm, did not convey anger or disapproval.

School policies are an important starting point for developing a whole school approach to generating good standards of behaviour and positive social attitudes. However, they are not much use unless all school staff, parents and children are aware of the policies and are actively involved in developing them.

A chance to think

Developing school policies is mainly the responsibility of the governing body. However, the governors and the headteacher should welcome discussion and comment on what policies on behaviour and bullying should contain, and on how the contents of the policies could be promoted.

Exercise 7.1

Look at your school's policies on behaviour and bullying and the contents of the home-school agreement. Make notes on how you would discuss these policies at a new parent's meeting of children about to enter the school. Do you think there is anything missing from the policies? What would you add? Would you change anything else about the policies? Discuss your notes with a colleague or mentor.

---

2. DEALING WITH CONFLICT

Conflict between individuals or groups within the school community can be a major source of disruption to the smooth and harmonious atmosphere in which children learn best. Dealing with conflict either between children or between you and a child is one of the most important skills for managing behaviour in schools.

Conflict is almost inevitable in any situation where there are a lot of children and adults together in an enclosed space. This is not peculiar to schools. Parents will often state that conflict between siblings is a major source of disruption in the home.

However, there are strategies for both reducing the chances of conflict developing, and dealing with conflict effectively when it arises, which can be learned and used with the children you work with. Conflict is not always a negative aspect of any group relationship. It can be used positively to air differing views and ideas and to create and promote debate. However, conflict can be damaging if it is mishandled or someone 'loses' or is hurt physically or emotionally.

2.1   What is conflict?

Conflict can be expressed verbally or physically, although sometimes it is not expressed at all. It is about the tension between two or more individuals, based on some form of disagreement. It can be temporary or long term and it can arise for all sorts of major or trivial reasons. Some children are more likely to be involved in open conflict than others. Some may appear never to get involved in conflict at all. The ways in which different children express conflict may depend on what they have learned from the adults around them and their own personality and characteristics. Conflict can be healthy, in terms of the expression of different viewpoints and the ability to express these. However, conflict can be damaging when it is expressed in personal terms, when it goes on over a period of time or when it involves harm to an individual.

2.2   Preventing conflict arising

We can never hope to eradicate conflict from the school altogether. However, it is possible to create an environment within school where conflict is reduced, where it is healthy, and where it is resolved quickly without harm to individuals. Whole school development is crucial to this process, based on promoting positive relationships between adults and children, founded on mutual respect and consideration. This type of development does not take place overnight but is part of a more general ethos which needs to be constantly renewed and reviewed. Some elements of this whole school ethos could include:

- Developing good relationships with children through communication, active listening and an interest in the individual child.

- Showing respect for all children and adults within the school.

- Taking action to reduce racism and discrimination within the school.

- Fostering a climate in which children are encouraged to help and support fellow pupils and adults model this behaviour.

- Creating and promoting clearly defined standards of behaviour and ensuring that these are part of the high expectations of children in the school.

- Developing strategies to deal with unacceptable behaviour and applying these in a timely and consistent way.

- Involving parents in discussions and strategies to develop the whole school ethos.

It is vitally important that you model these types of behaviour in your work with the children, demonstrating good practice in your relationships with others and a calm, problem-solving approach to any difficulties which arise. Receiving respect from others is important in building young children's confidence and their belief in themselves as valued beings; therefore it is important to maintain respectful relationships with the children you work with.

It is also important to consider your self-presentation. Children will respond better to adults around them who behave in authoritative ways and who present themselves as confident and coping. It helps to be firm and calm in your dealings with children and to demonstrate that you do not need to get angry or shout to ensure the children pay attention and respond appropriately to you. Positive, confident body language and open, confident facial expressions can reinforce an effective personal presence. A calm tone and relaxed manner can help children to learn to trust you and to gain respect for your authority.

A positive, problem-solving environment in school, in which opportunities are taken to discuss and explore difficult issues, either one to one or in circle time or assembly, will contribute to reducing the incidence of conflict. However, children bring many worries, problems and difficulties to school, as well as those that develop at school, and inevitably some conflict will arise.

2.3 Dealing with conflict in school

Conflict most commonly arises between children, but can arise between you and a child or children. Dealing with conflict between children needs patience, sensitivity and tact to ensure that positive solutions are found and implemented. Not all conflict requires adult intervention. Unless a child is becoming distressed or there is physical aggression it may be better on many occasions to let children work out their differences themselves. In this way, children learn about compromise and negotiation, controlling their stronger emotions and altruistic behaviour. It is important that young children have the opportunity to do this, as a significant contribution to their social development. Children of school age often have the skills and maturity to sort out short-term conflicts between themselves. However, adults should always intervene when:

- Conflict between the same individuals persists.

- There is bullying.

- Any child is becoming distressed or humiliated.

- There is physical aggression.

- Other children are becoming involved or distressed.

Strategies for intervention will obviously vary, depending on the situation, the age of the children and the type of conflict. Power-assertion techniques, such as shouting at the children, may be successful in the short term, but do not solve the longer-term problems that have caused the conflict in the first place. In order to do this, it is important to consider causes and motivations and to ensure that the outcomes of conflict resolution are going to be positive for all involved. A good solution is one where there are no 'winners' and 'losers' but where all involved gain from behaving in different ways.

There are a number of stages to dealing with conflict, which may include:

- Stopping aggressive verbal or physical behaviour and ensuring all children's safety as a priority.

- Communicating with the children about their behaviour and the reasons for it.

- Listening to the children and accepting their feelings about the situation.

- Looking for the underlying problems which are causing the conflict.

- Seeking solutions that help everyone involved to behave and feel better, and which reduce the chances of further conflict.

A chance to think

Resolving conflict requires an open mind and a calm and supportive approach. In order to solve longer-term conflict, it can be important to establish the facts and to discuss the issues and feelings underlying the incidents that have taken place. Telling children to behave in a different way or punishing them will not always resolve the problems between them.

Exercise 7.2

Read the case study and answer the following questions. Discuss your answers with a colleague or mentor, or compare them with the sample answers on pages 166–7.

1. What action would you take to resolve this conflict?

2. How would you try and help both children to better develop their social skills?

Chris and Harry

Chris and Harry, both 6, both white, have had a series of disagreements, loud arguments and tussles in the playground over the last two weeks. They have shouted at each other in the dining room and even in the classroom. The conflict has started to distress some of the other children in the class. It has been established that changes in friendship groups have left Harry feeling left out and vulnerable and he sees Chris as the child who is excluding him from group play. Chris feels that Harry is always trying to takeover his games, and play with the other children he regularly mixes with.

Children and adults may sometimes get into conflict and this may need dealing with in a similar way to conflict between children. If a child is angry or aggressive towards you, it is important to ensure that you:

- Remain calm and in control, never become aggressive yourself.
- Seek help if necessary.
- Talk to the child and listen to him/her.
- Acknowledge that the child is upset and try to encourage him/her to share his/her feelings.
- Try to remove yourself and the child to a quiet place.
- Try to get other children to move away.

It may be necessary to involve others in an incident to ensure that it does not escalate and that it is dealt with appropriately and within the law and policy guidelines. Teachers are permitted to restrain children physically in certain limited circumstances, to avoid harm to the child, other children or adults, or property. If a child becomes physically aggressive, it is very important to seek help immediately from the teacher and to ensure that other children are removed from the vicinity as quickly as possible. Any such incident should be recorded and discussed with the teacher and possibly the headteacher so that strategies to avoid a repetition can be developed, and parents informed.

2.4 Dealing with bullying

Not all conflict is mutual. In some circumstances, children are subject to bullying by another child or children. Bullying is common at all stages of school and has to be dealt with effectively to ensure that the bullied child does not suffer from long-term difficulties associated with the bullying. A whole school policy, which promotes positive relationships between children, and between children and adults, may make bullying less likely to take place. However, there is some bullying in most schools and this must be dealt with firmly.

Children who are bullied often lose confidence and self-esteem, possibly resulting in further bullying or escalation of bullying tactics. This loss of confidence can result in social isolation, which can be exacerbated if the bully or bullies are acting to isolate the child already. Bullied children can start to lose ground with their schoolwork, to refuse school, or even develop psychosomatic illnesses in order to avoid school. Not all bullying involves physical aggression. Often bullying involves a range of tactics designed to oppress and isolate the bullied child and to ensure that they do not feel safe within school. Common bullying behaviour includes:

- Verbal abuse or taunts.
- Racist remarks or remarks based on a child's physical or cultural features.
- Isolating a child, refusing to let them join in play or activities.
- Physical aggression or assault.
- Threats of physical aggression or assault.

Bullying is rarely a one-off incident. It usually involves a pattern of behaviour, often involving a number of children. The pattern is often complex and there are gender differences between how boys and girls bully. Most bullying is within the same gender, but how girls bully sometimes differs to how boys bully. Studies show that boys are more likely to be physically aggressive. Bullying between girls is more complex, sometimes taking place within apparent 'friendships'. For example, Lauren, 6, and Janey, 7, were apparently 'best friends'. However, Janey often threatened Lauren with the end of the friendship if Lauren did not do as Janey said, or if she played with other children. Lauren became very unhappy and upset that Janey seemed to be falling out with her all the time. Janey also threatened other children in the same way, so that Lauren felt isolated and had no one to play with. Lauren began to behave as if Janey could control all aspects of her life in school.

Bullying has to be dealt with within the school bullying policy, and it is important to be familiar with the contents of this policy. Bullying is not usually associated with one-off incidents, but involves a pattern of behaviour. It is important to communicate with the teacher about incidents you are aware of, so that bullying is detected at an early stage. It is common for bullied children not to report incidents or discuss the bullying with anyone. They may be subject to threats or feel confused or ashamed about what is happening to them. If you believe a child is being bullied, it is important not just to deal with the latest incident, but to ensure the teacher is aware that there have been a number of such incidents. Bullied children need reassurance and support from the adults around them, but most of all, they need to have the bullying stopped. Action to stop bullying may involve talking to the bully or bullies and explaining the consequences of their actions; whole class or whole school discussions on the unacceptable nature of bullying; arranging a 'circle of friends' for the bullied child; informing parents; and at the most extreme end, excluding the bullying child.

For example, when Sarah, seven, was bullied by three of her classmates, she did not tell anyone what was happening for several weeks. However, the lunchtime supervisors became aware that she was alone in the playground and clearly upset most days. Several incidents were reported, in which Sarah was verbally taunted by the other girls. They also taunted any other child who tried to play with Sarah, effectively 'scaring them off'. The teacher became aware of the bullying from the lunchtime supervisors and from comments from other children. She spoke to Sarah who confirmed what had happened. Sarah was clearly very distressed. The head-teacher was informed. She spoke to the girls involved and kept them in at lunch-time. They were asked to talk and write about how Sarah might feel. They were all sorry and ashamed about what had happened, and they wrote Sarah a note to apologize. All the parents were informed of the bullying and the action taken. Bullying was discussed as an assembly topic the following week.

Bullying is generally dealt with by class teachers or by the headteacher. However, you have a vital role in observing children's behaviour towards each other, communicating your concerns to the teacher, supporting the bullied child and dealing with incidents as they arise.

3. DEALING WITH OTHER TYPES OF UNWANTED BEHAVIOUR

In this section, we will explore effective responses to a range of more general unwanted behaviour in children. Racism and discriminatory behaviour will be dealt with in the following section. In order to provide children with an effective learning environment, there needs to be order and discipline in schools. Children should not be fearful or oppressed by rules and disciplinary measures, but should be taught to recognize the benefits of an orderly environment. Children learn positive social values such as self-discipline, concern for others, helpfulness and respect for others from being in a school where values are part of their wider learning. Discussions about values, what is expected and what is unacceptable, are part of the day-to-day learning about good behaviour which young children need.

Inevitably, there will be some unwanted behaviour among children in primary schools. Young children are still learning a great deal about accepted social behaviour at this age. There are many variations in the level of maturity among children in the infant stage. They may know what is expected of them but occasionally forget. They may be testing the boundaries to see if they are firm. They may be bored or tired, or upset about something at school or at home. They may be confused or uncertain about the activity they are supposed to be doing, or unable to understand what is expected of them. They may need help, but not feel confident about asking for it. Or they may want to attract more attention from other children or adults because they feel forgotten or ignored. The sorts of behaviour that are expected of children within the home also vary, so that there may be disparities between what is expected at home and school for some children.

There are many reasons why children behave in unwanted ways. There are also many different possible responses to unwanted behaviour, which may have different outcomes. It is important to recognize that most young children need support and help to behave well, rather than criticism, harsh discipline or condemnation. Some basic principles for dealing with unwanted behaviour include:

- Criticize the behaviour not the child.
- Explain to the child why the behaviour is not acceptable.
- Do not describe the child in negative terms e.g. 'silly girl'.
- Listen to the child's explanation.
- Use firm tones, but do not shout or raise your voice.
- Be clear about the behaviour that is expected.
- Praise and encourage desired behaviour to help children understand what is expected of them and to 'reward' them for meeting those expectations.
- Do not humiliate the child in front of others.
- Make sure the reprimand or punishment is proportionate to the level of unwanted behaviour, and not excessive or unkind.
- Be fair and consistent.
- Deal with the behaviour at the time, not later.

3.1 Types of unwanted behaviour

The sorts of behaviour which are unwanted in young children in school are those which:

127

- Are disruptive to the learning process.

- Threaten the health and safety of children or adults.

- Distress, embarrass or upset other children or adults.

- Involve verbal or physical abuse of another child or adult.

Typical examples of some of these are:

- During 'carpet time' Ryan ties his shoelace to that of the child next to him, creating a domino effect so that after twenty minutes four children are shackled together.

- During whole class teaching in literacy hour, Hannah leans forward and starts to twiddle with the hair of the child in front of her, distracting about five other children in the process.

- During silent reading, several boys gather at the shelves to 'change their books', and instead start to chat among themselves about toys.

- Kay and David reach for the same pencil at their table and then start a loud squabble about who should have it, culminating in pushing and shoving each other off their chairs.

- At dinnertime, Dan leaps out of the queue for lunches and entertains the other children by dancing round, pulling faces and blowing 'raspberries', until the queue collapses.

- Karen and Shiraz, both 7, rampage around the playground play-fighting with each other, shouting at the top of their voices, oblivious of others until they flatten a smaller child.

- Supposedly absorbed in completing drawings of different types of dwelling places, Mark entertains his table by drawing pictures of 'willies'.

- Cheryl asks Tom to pass her a rubber, instead he throws, she catches and tosses it back and so on.

- Harry refers to the child next to him as 'you prat'.

- Fauzia and Jane follow the lunchtime supervisor down the playground doing an exaggerated imitation of her walk.

3.2 Strategies for dealing with unwanted behaviour

Dealing with unwanted behaviour requires patience, tact, firmness and fairness. The object is to minimize the disruption caused by the behaviour and to discourage the child or children from repeating it. In some cases, the child or children may need to be made aware of the distress they have caused and to make reparation, usually apologies. Children respond best to disciplinary measures from adults who they respect and feel positive about. Possible strategies include:

- Verbal reprimands, delivered in a calm, but very firm tone.

- Ignoring minor incidents of unwanted behaviour, in the context of praising wanted behaviour.

- Explaining to the child why their behaviour is unacceptable, dangerous or hurtful to others.

- Suggesting alternative ways of behaving.

- Removing the child from an 'audience' or removing the 'audience' from the child.

- Giving the child additional responsibilities or tasks to do to occupy him/her more.

For more serious incidents, you will need to report the behaviour to the teacher for consideration of further sanctions or punishments. However, it is important to be able to deal with incidents as they arise and to do this confidently and with authority.

A *chance to think*

Dealing with unwanted behaviour in young children can be challenging. Balancing the needs of the child with the needs of the wider school community requires a careful and considered approach. A child who is humiliated or embarrassed because he/she has been behaving in unacceptable ways is not less, but more, likely to repeat the behaviour. A child who is treated fairly and firmly will understand better what is expected of him/her and be more likely to want to improve his/her behaviour.

Exercise 7.3

Look at the examples of unwanted behaviour listed above. For each, describe how you might deal with the behaviour. Compare your ideas with those on pages 167–8.

Finally, it is important to remember that repeated and possibly escalating unwanted behaviour might be an indication of a deeper problem. Children who are abused or being bullied or who are worried or distressed may behave in unacceptable ways in order to draw attention to their plight. Children who have learning difficulties or special educational needs may be trying to distract others from recognizing their difficulties or gain the status they feel they cannot get through achievements in the classroom. Children going through changes at home, such as divorce or the birth of a new baby, may be expressing their uncertainty and anxiety. Any concerns about the possible causes of patterns of unwanted behaviour should be shared with a teacher who may then discuss these with parents.

4. DEALING WITH RACISM AND DISCRIMINATION

This type of unwanted behaviour has been dealt with as a separate section in order to underline the serious impact of racism and discriminatory behaviour on children who are subject to it. It is also discussed further in Chapter 8. For example, Leanne, 5, referred to her classmate Shabana as a 'Paki' in the classroom. It became clear that Leanne did not understand the meaning of the term, and that she had over-heard it in the playground, not at home. However, it was also clear that Leanne knew that this term was used of certain children and not others. Shabana, on the other hand, knew that this was an abusive term for British Asian children and was very upset. The question we need to consider first is how children learn this type of behaviour at such an early age.

The values of a society are passed to children through their experiences at home and school, and these shape the child's attitudes, values and beliefs about the world around them. These views of the world – cultural norms – are reinforced by the media (TV, cinema, newspapers and magazines, advertising) and by peers and other adults. Children learn that different values are placed on different groups and individuals in society. They also absorb the prejudices that are common within their own culture. 'Culture' means the sorts of customs and practices, beliefs and ideas of a particular group in society. In British multicultural society there is a dominant culture against which other cultural practices and beliefs are sometimes unfavourably compared.

Children also absorb the expectations of those around them. For example, there is no inherent reason why boys and girls should play with different types of toys, but children learn to do this in response to the expectations of those around them and the messages they receive about the sorts of toys that are appropriate to their gender. (Watch the adverts on TV during children's programmes in the run-up to Christmas to fully appreciate the influence of the media in this process!) (Kay, 2001).

Children also model their behaviour on that of the adults around them, absorbing negative messages about certain groups in society. Consequently, children with learning difficulties or physical disabilities, children from minority ethnic groups and children with family backgrounds which do not conform to cultural norms may be subject to particular types of bullying or abuse within schools. It is also important to remember that children within these groups may absorb negative messages about themselves, affecting their confidence and self-esteem. The effects of discrimination may be:

- Children may not reach their full potential.
- Low self-esteem may have a negative impact on the child's ability to form relationships.
- Children may have lack of confidence to experiment.
- Children may feel ashamed of their race and culture.
- Children may internalize negative views and feel as if they deserve poor treatment.
- The effects are lifelong.

(Tassoni, 1998: 11)

It is important to take any discriminatory behaviour very seriously in schools, and to recognize that it may have a different impact to more generalized bullying behaviour or conflict between children. For example, primary schools often promote multiculturalism through activities that explore the food, dress and habits of different cultures and celebrations of a range of different festivals and religious practices. It is important to recognize that this alone will not prevent racist behaviour in schools. Children may not make the links between the new information they have about a range of cultures and the discriminatory behaviour that is part of the society we live in.

Dealing with racism and discrimination against specific groups or individuals starts with whole school development, based on sound policies (David, 1993). These issues should be part of discussions within school and with parents. Children need to be made aware of the issues around discrimination, rather than just knowing that certain behaviour is not acceptable. In order to tackle racism and discrimination we need to:

- Become consciously aware of our own views and behaviour.

- Be able to discuss these issues with others.

- Be aware of relevant school policies.

- Be sensitive to the experiences of children who may be subject to discriminatory behaviour both inside and outside school.

- Develop an open mind and respect for the values and beliefs of others.

Some examples of this type of unwanted behaviour may include:

- Children choosing and rejecting playmates on the basis of ethnic origin or disability.

- Verbal abuse based on race or disability or learning difficulties.

- Physical abuse, threats or harassment based on these factors.

For example, Jason, 6, told Rahim, as the punch line to an argument, 'You're dad wasn't even born here, then!' Mary, 7, used the term 'mong' to refer to a child with learning difficulties, and Gary, 5, stated in the playground that he was not playing with any of 'them' clearly referring to a family of black children who had recently arrived in school.

It is not inevitable that racism and discrimination are rife in schools. Schools have a strong influence on the children in their care and the development of whole school approaches to these issues can be very positive in creating a supportive accepting environment for all children.

Strategies to deal with racism and discrimination include:

- Talking to both children with sensitivity and patience about the underlying issues.

- Being aware of repeated patterns of behaviour.

- Discussing incidents with the teacher.

- Participating in whole school activities aimed at tackling discrimination.

- Modelling positive behaviour.

- Supporting children who are subject to discrimination with positive statements and images of themselves.

5. HELPING CHILDREN TO LEARN EFFECTIVELY

Teaching assistants are often involved in supporting individual or small groups of children who may have particular problems or difficulties with their work or behaviour in school. There is a link between children's ability to confidently tackle tasks and their chances of achievement. Unwanted behaviour is often associated with children who are struggling to progress. Helping children to behave in more constructive ways may involve encouraging some changes in behaviour patterns that may have become established before the child arrived in school. Changing, or modifying, children's behaviour is not an instant process, but one that requires time, patience and commitment. However, it is important to recognize the role of adults in shaping children's behaviour and how this can be achieved most effectively.

Types of behaviour that may cause difficulties may include:

- Disrupting and distracting other children.

- Avoidance of activities and tasks.

- Failure to stay on task, poor concentration.

- Aggressive or hostile behaviour.

- Withdrawn and unresponsive behaviour.

- Failure to participate in whole class activities.

All children may display these types of behaviour at different times. This may be associated with tiredness, illness, problems at home or school or failure to understand what is required within a particular activity. However, some children may have developed patterns of these types of behaviour which may inhibit the progress of their learning. Reasons for this may include:

- Learning delays or difficulties.

- Physical disabilities or sensory impairments.

- Specific conditions e.g. autistic spectrum disorders.

- Negative feelings or beliefs about school.

- Poor early learning experiences.

- General developmental delays.

- Social problems or disadvantages.

- Emotional problems or developmental delays.

- Child abuse.

Helping children to learn effectively should always be part of a wider strategy to support them with problems or difficulties, and should be in the context of the child's Individual Education Plan (IEP) where appropriate. IEPs are plans that are drawn up for children where special educational needs have been identified. They include targets for progress with the child's learning development, which are reviewed regularly. IEPs are developed by the SENCO, in partnership with the parents, the teacher and any other professionals involved with the child. This could include an educational psychologist, LEA Advisory teacher, health professionals and you, as the child's support worker in school.

Helping children to change their behaviour to learn more effectively should always be based on clearly defined goals, which reflect an understanding of the individual child's needs. Often negative patterns of behaviour are associated with lack of confidence or poor self-esteem, which contribute to a feeling of failure in the learning environment.

6. STRATEGIES TO SUPPORT MORE EFFECTIVE LEARNING

Hurst and Joseph (1998: 30) argue that:

- Children's self-knowledge and sense of self-value grow from being treated respectfully by others who know them well.

- Children's own growing self-respect and self-knowledge enable them to respond to others with understanding and respect.

- Respect for their own capacities as learners and for others as learners enable children to come to discipline themselves for their own educational and personal benefit.

Strategies to support effective learning should always take into account the impact of adult behaviour on children's self-esteem and self-confidence, which continue to have a significant impact on their capacity to learn throughout childhood and beyond.

It is important to discuss strategies to support learning with the teacher and to contribute your own views based on your knowledge of the child. Different strategies may work with different children, so there may be an element of 'trial and error' in choices of approach. These could include:

- Giving praise and encouragement for achievements and for progress.

- Giving praise for wanted behaviour.

- Using clear, simple language to describe tasks and activities.

- Breaking tasks down into manageable stages.

- Repeating instructions to ensure they are clear.

- Differentiating tasks to match individual or small group needs.

- Revising activities to meet individual or small group needs.

- Modelling the approach to the task.

- Supporting the child in her work until she is ready to work more independently.

It is important that the child receives praise for genuine achievements, hard work or progress. Children quickly realize the low value of praise given for every piece of work they do, regardless of the amount of effort and attention which has gone in to it. High expectations of children are important in determining the child's self-esteem and confidence in tackling new tasks.

A chance to think

Supporting children in their work can be very rewarding when progress is made, and very frustrating when this does not happen. Children need to understand that you are there to help them develop the skills to tackle work. Activities need to be tailored to meet the needs of children, in terms of their ability and developmental stage. Asking children to tackle tasks that are beyond them, without appropriate support, will damage self-confidence. Giving praise for progress and improvements in the child's approach to learning is as important as giving praise for achievement. Read the case study below and make notes on how you would approach the task of helping the child with her writing. Describe the approach you would use, the activities and materials you consider may be most useful, and the methods you would use to promote positive learning behaviour.

Exercise 7.4

Beth, 6, is reluctant to tackle any writing activities at all. She has had problems learning sounds because of a slight hearing impairment, and although her reading is progressing, this has been slow. Beth has become conscious that she is not writing as well as the rest of the class, and this has resulted in a series of avoidance tactics. Given writing tasks to do, she will delay starting the task, ask to go to the toilet, walk around the room, change and fuss with her pencil and disrupt other children by chatting to them. Often she only produces a word or two, with a lot of help. You are going to work with her in literacy hour two mornings a week, to support her writing progress. Compare your ideas with the sample answers on page 169.

7. SKILLS FOR SUPPORTING CHILDREN'S LEARNING AND BEHAVIOUR

Working effectively to support children's learning and behaviour requires a range of interpersonal skills, including skills in communication, building relationship, controlling children's behaviour and managing the learning environment. You will probably have brought many of these skills to your job as a teaching assistant already. However, it is useful to be aware of the range of skills required and to develop self-awareness in terms of the areas of skills you are confident in and the areas of skills you need further development in. Broader professional skills will be discussed more fully in Chapter 8.

7.1 Communication skills

We are all aware that communication skills are important for working with children, but it is useful to consider for a moment exactly what type of communication skills are most helpful. Defining communication as the two-way transmission of messages reminds us that it is as important to listen to children, as it is to talk to them. Listening skills are crucial in both assessment of children's needs and our understanding of how to meet them. In Chapter 3, we looked at the development of listening skills as part of Key Stage 1 English. It may be useful to look back at the relevant section of Chapter 3 now, and to reread your notes for Exercise 3 within that chapter.

Listening requires us to concentrate on what the child is saying, but also to try and understand underlying messages within the communication, possibly conveyed through non-verbal media. For example, the child who says, 'I'm fine' although he looks miserable, speaks in a flat tone of voice, hangs his head and refuses to make eye contact. Listening is also a crucial part of building relationships with children, who always appreciate adults who are willing to spend time listening to them.

How we talk to children is also very important. It is almost astonishing at times how negatively adults speak to children. Harsh tones of voice, barked commands and shouting may satisfy the adult need to dominate the child, but are not much use in developing a positive learning environment. Children need adults to:

- Speak clearly in language they can understand.
- Explain carefully and check explanations are understood.
- Secure the child's attention before speaking.
- Repeat patiently if necessary.
- Use firm but friendly tones of voice.
- Speak firmly and confidently when giving instructions, particularly when maintaining control.
- Discuss and review work.
- Praise and encourage.
- Ask open-ended questions and extend discussions through questioning.
- Listen to the child's contribution and respond to it.

Speaking to children respectfully enhances rather than impairs adult authority. It also models this type of communication to the children. Good quality discussions are a key feature of successful learning for young children.

Non-verbal communication is a major tool in conveying meaning. Children are sensitive to the non-verbal messages they receive and may respond to these rather than the verbal message being given. For example, a student teacher was in charge of the Year 1 class on a Friday afternoon close to the end of term. The children were sitting on the carpet for quite a long period, and tired and fractious, they fidgeted and annoyed each other until a steady murmur disrupted the class. The student continued to speak in a soft voice, but her body posture became rigid and angry and her facial expression became grim. The noise level rose as the children became distracted and anxious about the level of anger and irritation they felt emanating from the student teacher. In the end, annoyed beyond endurance, she spoke loudly and sharply to two girls, who both promptly burst into tears.

Non-verbal communication should convey a strong message of confidence and authority to the children, through relaxed body posture, and a calm face and tone of voice.

7.2 Building relationships

In order to work well with young children individually or in groups, it is important to build relationships with them that are trusting and relaxed, through which the child can learn effectively and gain confidence. In order to build such relationships you need to be:

- Supportive, firm and patient.
- Committed to helping the child progress.
- Friendly, but not over-friendly.
- Able to respond to the child as an individual.
- Able to recognize and respond to the child's individual needs.
- Have high expectations of the child.
- Communicate effectively with the child.

Children develop their self-image through their perceptions of other people's views of them, therefore it is important to reflect back to them that they are valued and important people who have worthwhile contributions to make.

7.3 Management of the learning environment

Within the context of the planned curriculum activities, whether working with groups or individuals, you will need to manage relevant sections of the learning environment. Clearly, this process takes place in the context of the teacher's role of whole class management, and should be harmonious and complementary to this. Communication with the teacher is crucial to effective management of the learning environment, and a clear understanding of the learning outcomes and planned activities is required. However, within these parameters you will need to develop skills for managing the learning environment for which you are directly responsible. For example, if you are supporting a group requiring high levels of intervention within the class to complete a piece of written work relating to whole class reading, you will need to:

- Ensure the instructions are understood by all the children.
- Ensure relevant materials are available.
- Ensure the pace is appropriate to the task, the amount of time available and the needs of the children.
- Share your attentions between the different children according to need.
- Use open-ended questions to encourage children to extend their efforts.
- Ensure that the children are all working, not 'queuing up' for your attention or distracting each other.

- Give praise and encouragement as required.

- Ensure that you are able to give feedback on individual progress to the teacher.

You are aiming for a calm and industrious working environment in which children know what is expected of them and are working hard, are able to ask questions and get support, but can work independently as well. In order to achieve this, you will need to be managing the learning environment throughout the session. This involves:

- Monitoring all the children visually to ensure they are 'on task'.

- Moving between children in a fluid and responsive way.

- Explaining, encouraging and answering questions.

- Giving clear instructions and using questions to take the work forward.

- Presenting yourself as in control.

- Communicating high expectations to the children.

The ways in which the learning environment can be effectively managed obviously vary, depending on the activity in hand, the child or children, the whole class learning outcomes and your role within achieving these. However, it is important to consider how you manage your part of the process to ensure that learning takes place at the highest possible level.

CONCLUSIONS

Teaching assistants play an important role in whole school development towards a positive learning environment, both within and outside the classroom. The development of personal skills and strategies to promote good standards of behaviour and to deal with conflict, bullying, discrimination and racism is important for anyone working within the school community. We know that children learn best in orderly, well-managed environments. Teaching assistants need to be able to support the teacher in creating and maintaining an appropriate learning environment within the classroom. They also need to create and manage a positive learning environment within their own particular remit, working with groups and individual children. Children not only learn best in such an environment, but they also learn about positive social behaviour, consideration and respect for others and anti-discriminatory behaviour. Developing skills to manage behaviour and learning effectively, without the use of power-assertion (shouting, threatening, frightening) techniques, is a significant part of the teaching assistant's learning requirements.

NOTES FOR FURTHER READING

David, T. (ed.) (1993)
Educating our Youngest Children: European Perspectives.
London: Paul Chapman.

Hurst, V. and Joseph, J. (1998)
Supporting Early Learning.
Milton Keynes: Open University Press.

Kay, J. (2001)
Good Practice in Child Care.
London: Continuum.

Parker-Jenkins, M., Briggs, D., Taylor-Basil, V. and Hartas, D. (2001)
The Implementation and Impact of the Home–School Agreement in Derbyshire Primary Schools.
University of Derby, School of Education and Social Science, Research Centre for Education and Professional Practice Working Papers Series 1: No. 1.

Tassoni, P. (1998)
Child Care and Education.
Oxford: Heinemann.

CHAPTER 8

Personal and Professional Development

INTRODUCTION

The concept of personal and professional development relates to the activities and processes you are involved in that contribute to the development of your knowledge, skills and understanding of your role as a teaching assistant. These activities and processes can be formal, such as attending training courses and gaining qualifications, or they can be informal, such as developing your own range of reading, discussing issues with colleagues, thinking about your own practice and observing others.

The need for development is partly based on the view that job roles are not static or 'set in concrete', but that they grow and change over time, and staff must grow and change with them. The field of education is subject to a wide range of developmental influences, which have an impact on what we do and how we do it. These changes can be a result of legislation, new policies, new methods of working or approaches. Often these are responses to perceived problems with the status quo, or they may be as a result of research findings that confirm that it may improve the children's experiences and achievements if we work in new or different ways. Some changes are driven by the political agenda, which may redefine the goals of the educational process or set new and challenging achievement targets.

The best ways to provide for the education of young children is a contested issue, with a variety of viewpoints, some traditional and some emerging. These viewpoints may influence policy and practice, through legislation or new directives. In recent years, changes have been frequent, as social and political pressure has driven education services towards providing for higher levels of achievement among our younger children and better quality in service provision. Job roles and expectations of teaching assistants have developed accordingly. The current agenda for teaching assistants will involve an accelerated rate of change in the next few years and a radical change in the roles and responsibilities of teaching assistants in all schools.

Other issues drive the need for ongoing development. Many teaching assistants want to extend their understanding and knowledge in order to support children and the learning process more effectively. The personal satisfaction of improving our performance at work can be a powerful incentive for some. Others may want to progress into other job roles, promotion, or further training into a range of professional roles. Routes into becoming a qualified teacher are opening up for teaching assistants, partly driven by the teacher shortage in some areas. Teaching assistants are increasingly being seen as key professionals in the classroom and their roles and responsibilities are under scrutiny, in terms of extending and developing these to meet teaching and learning needs of all children.

Some teaching assistants may feel that they need to develop specific skills to meet the particular requirements of their post or the unique needs of the children they work with. For example, you may want or need to develop skills in sign languages such as Makaton, to communicate more effectively with some children with communication and learning difficulties; or to learn a second language to work more closely with multi-lingual children; or to find out more about the needs and requirements of children with autistic spectrum disorders. Other may have areas for development identified by colleagues or supervising staff, as part of a mentoring or appraisal process.

Whatever the reasons for personal development, it will be part of the work of every teaching assistant to identify and meet their own development needs and to ensure that their practice reaches a high standard and meets the requirements of their particular post.

A chance to think

The field of education is dynamic, with changes in policy and practice reflecting the search for higher standards and achievements. Changes in policy and practice can often seem imposed from 'on high' either by the school management, the LEA or the DfES. Responding to change can be challenging, with many school staff and others in education developing 'initiative burn-out' in response to the seemingly endless demands for development. It can be hard sometimes to see the link between new demands, policies and practices and a real change in quality. Some changes may seem to bring negative elements with them, or be incomprehensible. The rationale for the development or new demand may not filter down to individuals working in the classroom. So, does change improve the quality of children's experiences in school?

Exercise 8.1

Think back to your own experiences in primary school.
   What was it like?
   What do you think has changed?
   Have the changes benefited children and if so, in what way?
   How have relationships changed in schools between adults and children?
   Try to look at the past and present objectively and identify the impact of change on the children.
   Discuss your thoughts with a colleague or mentor. Ask a colleague who is of a different age to you to share his or her views on these questions.

This chapter explores the development of reflective practice as a skill for effective change and looks at some of the main areas of development relevant to the role of a teaching assistant.

1.	**REFLECTIVE PRACTICE**

Developing reflective practice is a key element of personal development. Reflective practitioners are those who ask the questions. 'Am I doing a good job?' and 'How can I do a better job?' of themselves, and then actively seek the answers. Reflective practice is the process of regularly reviewing our own work and the work setting and looking for improvements. Woods (1998: 27) describes reflective practice as 'the hallmark of the genuine professional'. She mentions several aspects of reflective practice for those working with young children:

- Theoretical understanding of childhood and child development.

- The ability to interlink theory and observations.

- Drawing 'valid and reasoned interpretations and assessments' from observations.

- Using these assessments to inform planning and practice with children.

The key issues are linking our day-to-day work practices to our understanding of theory and our knowledge of children's needs and how they can be met. We do this through the media of observation, discussion, reflection and then using our conclusions in planning for change. The knowledge we have informs practice and we judge our practice against what we know. We use this judgement or assessment to plan for improvements.

For example, if you are working one to one with a child who has difficulty concentrating, you may try different approaches to help the child focus on his/her work. The approaches you use will be informed by your knowledge of child development and the individual child. Observation will provide information on the most effective methods of helping the child concentrate, and from this you can judge the best approach. You can then plan how to develop the most effective approach to best support the child. However, it may be that you do not find an approach that helps the child concentrate better. You then may need to discuss this issue with colleagues, or read about it, or share your problem with a mentor or supervisor, to try and widen your knowledge and understanding to inform new approaches.

This process of using reflection to draw conclusions and plan for change is based on sound knowledge of developments in the field of education and a growing understanding of children's needs. However, we may ask how the changes in the field of education come about in the first place.

1.1 Theory and practice

The ways in which we support children's learning have changed radically from the rote teaching and learning of nineteenth-century elementary schools. The relationships between adults and children in schools have also changed radically over time, with increased emphasis on support and respect rather than the emphasis on power differentials and rigid control of children's behaviour. For example, in the author's primary school days, physical punishment of children, humiliation and sarcasm were accepted tools of the teacher's trade, but they would no longer be

141

considered acceptable now. The question you might ask is what drives these developments – what influences change? For example, the negative consequences of humiliating children and controlling them through intimidation have been recognized through the growth of the discipline of psychology, and the gradual increase in our understanding of children's emotional needs. Work on self-identity and self-esteem has shown that the ability to learn effectively is linked to good levels of self-confidence and high self-esteem. Educationalists recognize that for children to perform well in learning situations, we must support and promote their self-esteem, and as a result we behave differently to children now in schools than we did 30 or 50 years ago.

Change comes about in response to the development of new ideas and theories about the best way to educate children and support their learning. These ideas and theories come from research studies, observations and analysis of data related to the education process. Theories come from practitioners, academics and those involved in research across a range of backgrounds, including educationalists, psychologists and sociologists. Change is not instant, it is based on the build-up over a period of time of new information leading to new ideas, which are considered, written about, tried out and tested, modified and tested again. Change can come from practice and then be consolidated by legislative and policy development, or it can be imposed.

1.2   The teaching assistant as a reflective practitioner

Your role as a reflective practitioner can be developed in a number of ways. However, the key elements are a willingness to analyse work practices and reflect on areas for improvement. This should apply both to your own work and the school as a whole. You do not need to be an academic or a researcher to make vital contributions to development. All practitioners have a role to play in improving standards and quality. Some of the ways in which this can be done include:

- Keeping up-to-date with new developments through reading, discussion and attendance at staff development events.

- Developing analytical skills and a critical approach through appraisal of work practices, consideration of the effectiveness of policy and practice and sharing ideas about change with others.

- Observation and analysis of observational data to provide evidence for evaluating the effectiveness of work practices.

- Discussion about new developments with colleagues and others to clarify and extend your own ideas and thoughts.

- Contributing to debates in school meetings and venues outside school.

- Continuing your own professional development through courses and other development activities.

- Suggesting and introducing change with the agreement of colleagues and supporting colleagues through change.

This list may seem daunting, and it is not expected or possible for teaching assistants to become effective reflective practitioners overnight. However, the process of becoming a reflective practitioner underpins the specific developments you are involved in, either school-wide or personally. For example, if you feel you need to develop better communication skills, this can be supported by reflecting on your existing skills, the areas you need to develop, and the steps you need to take to achieve required changes.

A *chance to think*

No teaching assistant can reflect on every single aspect of his or her work on a daily basis. Much of your work will be done in a fairly automatic and unquestioning way, until perhaps, issues arise that demand a closer look at work practices. However, when we have to question or review work practices, we need the skills to do this constructively.

Exercise 8.2

Think of a work practice or routine in your workplace and ask yourself the following questions about it:

1. Is the practice effective in achieving aims?

2. Does it meet the children's needs?

3. Could it be done in a different way and would this be more effective and meet the children's needs better?

4. Is the current practice in line with what we know about best practice in the area?

Discuss your reflections with a colleague or mentor and ask for their views.

1.3   Getting support to become a reflective practitioner

There are a number of sources of support for teaching assistants to become more effective reflective practitioners. These include:

- Sharing ideas and discussing them with more experienced others.

- A mentor or peer who is available to discuss issues with you on a regular basis.

- Good use of appraisal and staff development opportunities.

- Attendance at meetings and training days.

- A school culture which promotes development for all staff.

Depending on your specific job role, some of you may have attended an LEA 'Induction Course for Teaching Assistants' based on DfEE (September 2000) guidelines found in the *Teaching Assistant's File – Induction Training for Teaching Assistants*. This course lasts for a total of four days and is based on materials contained within the file. The course covers many similar areas to this book, including maths and literacy, behaviour management and general background, as well as an introduction to the school. However, just as importantly, the course and the materials are designed to promote a reflective approach to your work, including a section in the file, the 'Reflective Notebook', which is available for you to add your own notes, observations and reflections on your work. If you have access to this course, it is a useful starting point to developing a reflective approach to your own practice, and should be used as such.

Developing reflective practice is an important stepping-stone to developing a wider range of skills, understanding and expertise. There are a number of areas of personal and professional development that are specifically relevant to the role of the teaching assistant, where development should be taking place on an ongoing basis.

2. ANTI-DISCRIMINATORY PRACTICE

Anti-discriminatory practice is about the development of ways of working that promote equality of opportunity and avoid discrimination (different or unequal treatment) between different children and their families. Anti-discriminatory practice includes not behaving in a discriminatory way and also actively supporting children and their families to try and overcome the impact of discrimination in other areas of their lives. In order to be effective in our anti-discriminatory practice, it is important to understand the roots of discrimination and how prejudice can influence our behaviour in subtle but powerful ways. Anti-discriminatory practice can be misunderstood at times, by focusing entirely on race and ignoring the other bases for discrimination that are common in our society. Or it can be seen as treating everyone in the same way, and therefore ignoring different needs. Sometimes practitioners can feel unsure about what is expected in terms of anti-discriminatory practice because they are unfamiliar with the concepts, the terminology, or their own real feelings. Millam (1996: 2) gives several reasons why discussing anti-discriminatory practice can feel uncomfortable:

- Lack of understanding of the issues and terminology.

- Feeling it is not appropriate to discuss this issue with small children.

- Anxiety about 'getting it wrong' or upsetting people.

- Not knowing where or how to start tackling these issues.

- Anxiety about addressing own attitudes and prejudices.

Although these are valid areas of concern, which need to be considered, they should not deter practitioners from becoming actively involved in anti-discriminatory practice at all levels. The opportunity for all children to reach their full potential is impaired by the discrimination some children encounter both within and outside the education system.

2.1 The bases of discrimination

Discrimination is rooted in the prejudices or assumptions held towards certain groups and individuals within a society. These prejudices are based on negative stereotypes about those groups or individuals which dominate the view of them and prevent a more balanced perception. These stereotypes are fixed and difficult to change, reflecting a strong belief system which may persist even when facts prove them to be illogical. For example, the author was teaching a class of adults about racial discrimination and its impact on young children. A mature student argued that his negative view of non-whites was justified by the impact of immigration on employment in the area. His perception that 'they' had taken all the jobs was unshaken by evidence that the non-white population in the area was less than 2 per cent.

Often those expressing strong prejudices will select information to support their views and ignore other information about the groups and individuals of which they have negative stereotypes. Therefore, differences are emphasized and similarities ignored. This has implications for multi-culturalism in schools, which will be discussed later.

Prejudices alone will not cause much harm, but when behaviour towards individuals is based on prejudices then it can become discriminatory. The main groups suffering from discrimination in Western societies are:

- Cultural and ethnic minorities.

- People with disabilities.

- Women and girls.

- Gays and lesbians.

- Older people.

This list is not exhaustive and many other small groups suffer discrimination at different times. Targets for discrimination can change or develop over time. For example, there have been a number of examples recently of discriminatory behaviour towards asylum seekers in the UK.

There are a number of different theories which seek to explain why certain groups are targets for negative stereotypes that lead to prejudice and discrimination. These include:

- Socialization of children into ways of thinking and viewing the world, which include negative stereotypes.

- Adults modelling behaviours which children then adopt.

Negative stereotypes are often rooted in history, and then perpetuated as part of the dominant culture through the mechanisms described above. It is not clear why levels of prejudice differ between individuals and groups or why certain groups are targeted by negative stereotypes in the first place. However, prejudices are often supported and perpetuated by the media and through other mechanisms by which the dominant culture is maintained.

2.2   Discrimination in practice

Discrimination may take the form of actions or behaviours by an individual or group towards those they are prejudiced against, or it may be institutionalized or part of the structure of an organization. This means that discrimination is built into how the organization operates. It may be overt, as in obvious, or covert, as in concealed.

Discrimination may affect children in schools because of their race or culture, their level of ability, their gender or social background. Children absorb the cultural messages about themselves and others, which are part of their socialization experiences. For example, Milner (1983) found that children as young as 3 years-old are able to understand the meaning of skin colour differences and to see white as preferable to black. Children may learn to feel inferior because of their skin colour or disability or family lifestyle. For example, African-Caribbean children do less well in school than any other group. The low expectations teachers had of black children were cited as one contributory factor in the Swann Report (DES, 1985). The effects of racism and ways of responding to racism are discussed in more detail in Chapter 7.

2.3 The role of teaching assistants in anti-discriminatory practice

Each school has an equal opportunities policy, which states the school's aims in terms of providing equality of experience for all children and adults within the school. This document should be part of the induction process of all staff and should be available for reference. Sadly, this is not always the case. Equal opportunities policies are statements of intent and it is important that they are reviewed to monitor progress. Some organizations are moving towards setting achievable targets for change as opposed to statements of intent in recognition of the dynamic progression towards higher levels of equality.

Teaching assistants often work with some of the most disadvantaged children within the school, supporting children with learning and physical disabilities, and working with individual and groups of children who have learning delays or who need extra support to learn effectively. Often children who are disadvantaged socially and economically are over-represented in this latter group. As such, teaching assistants are ideally placed to contribute significantly to the development of anti-discriminatory practice within the school. However, the teaching assistant's role must be based on relevant knowledge, skills and understanding in areas such as those described below:

- An understanding of the meaning of the terms 'equality of opportunity' and 'anti-discriminatory practice'.
- An understanding of the links between stereotyping, prejudice and discrimination.
- Knowledge of the bases of discrimination in British society.
- Knowledge and understanding of the effects of discrimination on some children.
- A belief that not all children have the same advantages.
- A belief that to some extent you can make a difference to this.
- Skills in challenging adults and children who express discriminatory views about others.
- Skills in developing themes in your work which support all children's sense of individual value and uniqueness.

- Knowledge and understanding of cultures other than your own.

- Understanding of the impact of a range of disabilities on children's lives.

- Gender issues and the outcomes of gender bias in the early years.

- Knowledge of your own prejudices and the ability to face and challenge these.

(Kay, 2001: 49)

Many schools emphasize a multi-cultural approach to cultural diversity to acknowledge and celebrate cultures other than the dominant white culture. However, this approach may be limited in developing a real understanding of a range of cultures. Representations of traditional costumes, food and festivals may be a good introduction to a range of cultures, but may also fail to help children learn cultural tolerance and acceptance of differences. At worst, it may reinforce stereotypes. Derman-Sparkes *et al.* (1989) warns us that we should avoid the 'tourist approach' to other cultures, because it merely emphasizes the difference between people, not the similarities.

Teaching assistants can support children by avoiding stereotypical assumptions about them and by showing a genuine interest in their particular family and life-style. Acknowledging differences and sharing similarities is an important part of this process. Recognizing each child as an individual is important, as is supporting children's positive views of themselves. It is also important to be honest with children, acknowledging and responding to difficulties and the impact of discrimination on their lives. For example, we should never assume that being 'colour blind' is an effective contribution to tackling racial discrimination. It is also important to extend knowledge and understanding of the bases of discrimination and their impact on children. Some of the ways this can be done is through:

- Talking to children and parents sensitively about their experiences.

- Reading about different cultures and disabilities.

- Talking to colleagues and friends about these issues.

- Keeping an open mind and a deep respect for the value and beliefs of others.

- Attending staff development events relevant to the issues you are dealing with in school.

It is also important to recognize that chastising children for discriminatory behaviour will not have a long-term effect on changing such behaviour. Talking to children about how their behaviour affects others and why they should behave differently is an important part of the process of change.

A chance to think

Discussing problems that occur and comments that are made can be a useful starting point for developing children's understanding of discrimination and the impact of discrimination on individuals. Using situations that arise to develop more general themes can sometimes be more useful than focusing entirely on the behaviour of one child.

> ## Exercise 8.3
>
> Today you overheard Eddie, 7, calling Gavin a 'spaz' in the classroom. When asked about this behaviour, Eddie said that he didn't know what the word meant, but that his friend Kevin had called Gavin the same name. Eddie said he was sorry, but was clearly unsure what he was supposed to be sorry about.
>
> What steps should be taken next and who should be involved?
>
> How could Gavin be supported in this situation?
>
> Discuss your views with a colleague or mentor and compare them with the sample answers on page 169.

Language is a key issue in anti-discriminatory practice. The way we speak to children, the language used and the different approaches to different children convey clear messages. For example, use of gendered language can imply that different behaviours are expected of boys and girls. If we refer to doctors, fire-fighters, police officers as 'he' we are telling our girls in subtle, but meaningful ways that these jobs are not for them. If we refer to children in terms of a difficulty, characteristic or disability they have, then we are defining them by this factor and not as a unique child. Referring to the 'child with learning difficulties' or the 'deaf child' merely reinforces negative stereotypes and self-image.

Children who are perceived as different may be more susceptible to bullying and have lower self-esteem and poorer self-confidence than other children. Being defined as 'different' may result in discrimination based on a wide range of reasons. Supporting all children in a safe, non-discriminatory environment requires a shared view of how this is to be achieved, which is clearly conveyed to children and parents. Teaching assistant's have a key role in developing this ethos and ensuring that all children benefit from it. Mutual respect, shared decision-making and clear codes of conduct are all part of such an ethos and depend on adults willing to discuss and share ideas about issues with children in a calm, confident and constructive manner. The teaching assistant's role is to ensure that their own knowledge and understanding of discrimination and anti-discriminatory practice provides a sound basis for effective practice in this area.

3. | CONFIDENTIALITY

Confidentiality is central to good standards of professional practice within schools, and yet levels of confidentiality can vary enormously and breaches of confidentiality can be common. Schools obtain a great deal of information about children and their families, some of which is highly sensitive. Confidentiality is about the ways in which this information is appropriately handled, stored and transmitted while ensuring that it both effectively informs work practices and is kept within boundaries of 'need to know'. On the surface this appears to be a fairly straightforward process, but in practice there are areas of uncertainty, particularly in relation to the limited circumstances in which confidentiality should be broken.

Confidentiality is one of the bases of trust between professionals, children and their families, and as such is an area where professional standards are judged by parents. No parent wants to feel that their personal circumstances or events in their family are up for gossip or speculation. Yet parents will often want to share information with schools in order to ensure that their child gets the right types of support and help. The concept of confidentiality is based on the rights of the child and the family to respect, privacy and sensitivity. It is closely linked to anti-discriminatory practice and good quality provision of education.

A *chance to think*

At times, we have probably all heard staff and others sharing information and bits of gossip about families in an unconsidered and inappropriate way. We may think that because parents have shared some pieces of information about their child or family circumstances with the school, that this means the information is not confidential. But there is a big difference between discussing details of, say, your divorce, with a teacher, and having it bandied round the staffroom as local gossip.

Exercise 8.4

Think of your own and your family circumstances.

Which issues would you be willing to share with others?

What would you prefer others not to know?

Are there any sensitive or painful issues you would really not want anyone to be party to?

How would you feel if you thought that you and your family were being discussed in terms of these issues?

Discuss your thoughts with a colleague or mentor.

Schools have a great deal of information about children and families. Normally, this is shared with staff on a 'need to know' basis, which means that some information you have should not be shared with others. Other information will be offered directly to you by parents or the child, and you may or may not feel this should be shared with others. There are some simple questions to ask yourself, which may help to decide whether information should be shared or not:

- Has this information been passed to you in confidence?

- Do you need to share this information to help the child?

- Is the information sensitive?

- Have you had permission to pass the information on?

- Who needs to know?

- Does the information relate to any problems with the child's safety or welfare?

If the answer is 'yes' to the last question, you may be in a position where it is necessary to breach confidentiality. This should only happen where the safety or welfare of the child is at risk if you do not breach confidentiality. The most common reason for this is in cases where there is suspected child abuse. If you come across information that relates to possible abuse of a child, then it is imperative that this is shared with an appropriate person. This could be the teacher, but if there is a great deal of importance resting on this confidence, you may wish to discuss this with the Child Protection Liaison Teacher, who has a role dealing with child protection issues within the school. Clearly, it is important to tell the parent or child who has given you the information that you must pass it on. Making promises to keep secrets that you cannot honour will only result in damage to trust. The Department of Health 1999 guidelines *Working Together to Safeguard Children* emphasize this point and advise anyone working with children that if child protection issues arise, confidentiality cannot be kept.

Recording and storage of information should be subject to the rules of confidentiality to ensure that access is only available to those who should have it. This means not leaving notes lying around at home and work, or in the car, and not letting others have access to them unless this has been agreed. Apart from the circumstances described above, in which confidentiality should be breached, information should only be shared with other agencies where this has been previously agreed, and then it should be shared in a format that has also been agreed. If in doubt, check with the teacher first and ensure that you are following agreed procedures for information about a particular child.

On some occasions you may come across information which should not be shared with anyone. A parent may tell you something highly confidential because they trust you and need someone to talk to. In this case, it is important to maintain confidentiality and share the information with no one, unless permission has been given, and unless there are risks to the child as discussed above.

Finally, it may be tempting at times to want to talk about different issues to do with work with your family or friends. Work can be stressful and tiring and may leave us emotionally and physically drained. Sometimes it is nice just to 'offload' on our nearest and dearest. It is at times like this that we need to be very careful about not breaching confidentiality and passing on information that should be kept to ourselves.

4. COMMUNICATION SKILLS

Developing good communication skills is a central area of professional development for anyone working with other people. Listening and communicating effectively with children, parents and colleagues is a key element of good practice in schools. Yet often we fail to listen to children and recognize their specific needs and communications. Communication skills and interpersonal skills for working with children are discussed in more detail in Chapter 7. However, it is also important to develop communication skills for working with parents and colleagues as well. Being a good listener and communicating clearly are key skills to develop within your job role. Developing communication skills depends on the ability to:

- Listen carefully and respond to others' communications.

- Consider our responses to achieve the communication we want to.

- Vary communication style and approach depending on the audience.

- Use language clearly and effectively and vary the language used to meet the needs of the listener.

- Be tactful, sensitive and maintain confidentiality.

Taking time to listen to parents and colleagues may seem difficult within a busy schedule, but it may well be crucial to good working relationships and positive support for others. It is important to ensure that we use positive non-verbal messages to others as well as good verbal communication. Listening attentively, focusing on the speaker and taking time to consider our responses are all positive tools in communication. Good working relationships between teachers and teaching assistants are built on and maintained by effective communication skills.

5. | WORKING WITH PARENTS AND OTHER PROFESSIONALS

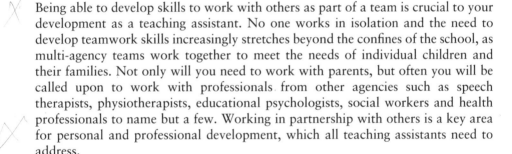

Being able to develop skills to work with others as part of a team is crucial to your development as a teaching assistant. No one works in isolation and the need to develop teamwork skills increasingly stretches beyond the confines of the school, as multi-agency teams work together to meet the needs of individual children and their families. Not only will you need to work with parents, but often you will be called upon to work with professionals from other agencies such as speech therapists, physiotherapists, educational psychologists, social workers and health professionals to name but a few. Working in partnership with others is a key area for personal and professional development, which all teaching assistants need to address.

5.1 Working with teachers

Clearly, the main relationship any teaching assistant will have is with the classroom team, mainly the teacher and any other classroom assistants. The DfEE guide *Working with Teaching Assistants* states that the relationship between teacher and teaching assistant is at the heart of the role of the teaching assistant and that failure in the relationship will impair the effectiveness of the teaching assistant to fulfill that role (DfEE, October 2000: 24). Factors that influence the quality of this relationship include:

- The extent to which the teaching assistant is involved in planning.

- The extent to which the teaching assistant is confident to act independently.

- Good feedback between the teacher and teaching assistant.

- Clear communication about behaviour management and the needs of individual children.

- The extent to which teaching assistants are included in IEP reviews, staff meetings and staff development.

- Open communication between the teacher and the teaching assistant about their relationship and how it may impact on children's learning.

This is not a relationship you can develop single-handedly – the teachers that you work with are part of this process too. However, teaching assistants can contribute a great deal to developing effective working relationships with teachers by developing and using good communication skills; becoming reflective practitioners and sharing their reflections; by making suggestions and sharing ideas about support for individual children, planning and review of lessons; and by showing confidence and independence in their work with children and relationships with adults within the school community. Not all your relationships with teachers will be the same, some will be easier and more effective than others. Some may be frustrating or difficult. Maintaining a professional approach and developing and demonstrating your skills is important in all situations, whatever the teacher's response. Good communication, openness and confidence are key skills for improving and developing better working relationships with colleagues. It is important to take the initiative and not wait for more senior colleagues to 'make it work'. Working with teachers is discussed more in Chapter 1.

5.2   Working with other professionals

Working with Teaching Assistants also emphasizes the importance of the relationship between teaching assistants and other professionals. With reference to the relationship between teachers, teaching assistants and other specialist staff the guidelines state: 'It is important to the welfare of the pupil that the connections between these three are smooth and that there are no inconsistencies or wasted initiatives because of poor communication' (DfEE, October 2000: 28).

Often teaching assistants are involved in implementing programmes for children in school, such as speech therapy or physiotherapy, which are designed and instigated by other professionals. Good communication, planning and review are important factors in ensuring this process works. For example, Kerry, 6, was identified as needing physiotherapy as part of a paediatric assessment. The physiotherapist met with the two teaching assistants involved with the child and Kerry's father at the school and trained them in a programme of exercises, designed to support the child's physical development. The teaching assistants and the father agreed a shared daily programme, clearly defining their different responsibilities. The teaching assistants kept a record of the exercises achieved daily and how well Kerry was progressing. A copy of this record was sent home weekly. The programme was reviewed at Kerry's IEP review meeting. The teaching assistants needed to communicate effectively both with other professionals, the teacher and the parents, and each other, in order to ensure the programme worked well and Kerry's needs were met.

Problems may arise in working with other professionals when there is a lack of clarity about different roles and responsibilities or where you are unclear about the other professional's role with the child and/or family. It is important to seek clarification and to ask questions about areas you are unsure of. Having a clear, shared idea of the goals you are working towards is vitally important. You also need to know:

- Specific responsibilities you may have towards the child.

- Any monitoring role you may have.

- Who you are expected to report to.

- The comparative roles of yourself and the teacher.

- Mechanisms for all professionals involved with the child to communicate with each other and the parents.

Communication is often routed through review meetings. It is important that you attend these where possible, or arrange to have your views expressed and to get feedback from the meetings that you cannot attend. If the child has an IEP, targets should be recorded and different roles and responsibilities described in this, so it is important that you have access to a copy of this for every child with SEN with whom you work.

5.3 Working with parents

Working with parents is another important role for teaching assistants. Parents are the first and most significant experts on their children and listening to their views and opinions can give an enormous amount of insight into a child's needs and how to meet them. The value of partnership with parents has been recognized within the education services for children of all ages. A co-ordinated approach to meeting children's needs that is free from conflict and which aims towards common goals is in the best interests of the child. This type of approach has special importance for children with SEN, where co-operation between professionals and parents is vital. Research in schools supports this view. For example, Bastiani (1995: 7) states: 'There is a clear argument, supported by extensive and convincing evidence, that the most effective education occurs when families and schools work together, as part of a shared enterprise.'

Parents, as mentioned earlier in this book, are defined as anyone who has parental responsibility for a child or care of the child. This could include mothers and fathers, foster carers, grandparents, step-parents or guardians. You may find that parents approach you in preference to the teacher, or that they may find you more accessible than the teacher. You may develop close relationships with parents when working one to one with a child with SEN. Providing a channel of communication for parents is an important function of the teaching assistant. However, there are pitfalls. Parents who are unhappy about their child's progress or some other aspect of the school, may use you as someone to complain to about the school, the teacher or even other children or parents. It is important to ensure that while giving such parents a sympathetic hearing, you do not let professional standards slip and give the impression that you are 'taking sides'. Some complaints may have value and some may just be 'offloading'. Whichever, you need to ensure you share any parental grievances with the teacher and agree a mutual response.

Communications with parents can be difficult at times. It may seem that you are subject to what feels like a great deal of unnecessary complaint. Developing good listening skills may help you recognize the deeply-felt anxiety and concerns that lie beneath an apparent barrage of complaint. Responding with sympathy and concern, acknowledging the anxiety and fears, and listening attentively can be very supportive for the parent. Often parents just need someone with whom to share concerns, and active listening is an effective tool in helping them feel that you have been supportive. Active listening may also help you to recognize problems or difficulties that need addressing in practical ways, which may not necessarily be clearly expressed.

Difficulties in developing good relationships with parents may be rooted in poor communication, cultural and language difficulties or negative parental attitudes to school and the education process. It is important to make efforts to communicate effectively and to understand the parents' views. For some parents, coming into school may bring back negative feelings about their own educational experiences and they may appear uncommunicative and even hostile. Presenting these parents with a calm, friendly, professional approach, listening to them and trying to communicate effectively with them may go a long way to helping them relax and start to co-operate in their children's educational processes.

6. | HEALTH AND SAFETY

Health and safety are the responsibilities of everyone who works in a school or any other environment in which children are cared for. The responsibility to keep children safe from harm overwhelms all other considerations. Young children need guidance on safe behaviour, they need support and monitoring, and they need help if accidents or damage occur. Children can never be made absolutely safe, but anyone caring for them has a clear duty to minimize the risks and ensure maximum safe behaviour. There is always a balance associated with this between children's needs for safety and security, and their needs for independence, exploration and play. For example, if we wanted children to be totally safe from knocks and bruises, we would never let them out at break. However, children have other needs, emotional, social and psychological, which could remain unmet if we suffocate them with too much care. In this section, we will explore safety issues and your duties to keep children safe and deal with any safety emergencies. At the end of each sub-section there is a checklist of points for action for you to use as reference or self-development. There is also a checklist in Section 3.5 of the *Teaching Assistant's File* (DfEE, September 2000), which is useful for those who may have access to it.

6.1 Health and safety regulations

The Health and Safety Act, 1974, and subsequent regulations, make it the responsibility of all employees to be aware of safety issues and to respond appropriately to them. They also place responsibility on employers to keep you safe. The regulations should be clearly displayed in the school and their guidelines followed. Specific requirements are that all equipment should be used safely and in accordance with instructions, and reporting any damage or hazards. Health and safety regulations are usually supported by specific policies relating to different aspects of health and safety within the school. It is important that you become familiar with these as well as the more general statements.

> *Points for action*
>
> 1. Check the location of the health and safety regulations within your school and ensure you are familiar with them.
>
> 2. Locate and read the school policies on health and safety and ask for clarification as required.
>
> 3. Find out who is the school safety officer and what their role is.

6.2   Accidents and health emergencies

Most accidents are avoidable if planning and organization have been effective and the layout of indoor and outdoor space and the use of equipment have been carefully considered. However, accidents and health emergencies do occur and you should be prepared for this eventuality. You need to have information about potential risks to certain children such as allergic reactions, chronic illnesses or specific conditions. Some allergies, for example, are potentially life-threatening, and you need to know if a child is at risk. In cases where it has been agreed that children bring medicines to school, these should be administered in accordance with the instructions and kept in a safe, locked location between doses. Any side-effects or contraindications should be discussed and a plan of action made for if problems occur.

In the case of an accident, first aid is usually applied by a trained first-aider within the school. You may consider training yourself, and this may be part of your job role. If a child is hurt, you need to be aware of how to contact a first-aider and where first-aid materials are located. It may be the school policy to allow all staff to treat very minor cuts or bruises. You may have to send another adult or an older child to get help if necessary or you may need to take the injured child to the medical room. It is important to stay calm and be reassuring after an accident and to ensure that the child is kept warm, still and calm, if there is any concern about serious injury or shock.

It is important to record injuries, in case there are complications later on, and to inform parents in writing so they are aware of any possible aftermath. A 'bump note' is usually completed and sent home with the child. This is particularly important with head injuries, which may result in concussion, the symptoms of which may appear quite a long time after the accident took place.

> *Points for action*
>
> 1. Check procedures for the event of a child being injured, including procedures for recording and for informing parents.
>
> 2. Make sure you know who the school first-aiders are and the procedures for locating them.
>
> 3. Check if you are allowed to give first-aid and in what circumstances.
>
> 4. Check the location of first-aid equipment.

> 5. Find out how information about risks to specific children is disseminated among staff and familiarize yourself with this information at regular intervals.

6.3 Illness and infection

It is important to recognize and respond to symptoms of illness in a child. You need to be aware of the procedures for monitoring and dealing with a child who has become ill in school, including the procedures for seeking treatment when parents cannot be located. Children who become ill in school should be taken to a warm, comfortable place where their condition can be monitored until a decision is made about what should happen next. If you are concerned about a child, you should mention this to the teacher immediately, or seek the advice of a first-aider. It is important to remain calm and comforting, especially with the youngest children who may become distressed or frightened about becoming ill in school.

Opportunities for the spread of bacterial infections should be reduced by maintaining good standards of hygiene, and taking safety precautions during activities such as cooking. Children should be encouraged to wash hands after using the toilet and before cooking or handling food, and they should be encouraged to use tissues and cover their mouths when coughing.

You also need to be aware of the symptoms of meningitis and respond immediately if a child is displaying these. Meningitis is a potentially life-threatening illness and the symptoms can develop very rapidly.

> *Points for action*
>
> 1. Check the procedures for dealing with sick children in school.
>
> 2. Check the guidelines for activities such as cooking.
>
> 3. Find and familiarize yourself with the information about meningitis and how we should respond to possible symptoms of this illness.

6.4 Creating a safe environment

Many accidents can be avoided by creating a safe environment for the children. Basic safety precautions are the responsibility of all staff and it is important that you do not assume that someone else will take care of any safety hazards in the indoor or outdoor environment. It is important to be vigilant about safety hazards such as evidence of electrical faults (frayed flexes, sparks from sockets); access to toxic substances (cleaning fluids, glue, polish); access to sharp objects; messy rooms; blocked corridors; and hazardous objects children may bring to school. School rules are often designed to promote a safe environment and children should be encouraged both to keep the rules and to understand why this is necessary.

All schools have security procedures to restrict access to the building and to ensure the building is secure during and after school time. It is important to know the procedures for ensuring children are secure within and outside the building, what to do if security is breached and systems for security after hours. Children must be prevented from leaving the premises by themselves or with unauthorized adults. It is very important that you feel confident to politely but firmly question any adult found on the premises who is not apparently with a staff member.

> ### Points for action
>
> 1. Check to whom you should report any potential safety hazard.
>
> 2. Check the procedures for dealing with a potentially hazardous object brought to school by a child.
>
> 3. Read the school rules and reflect on how they relate to safety issues.
>
> 4. Check the procedures for locking up, setting alarms and restricting access to the school.
>
> 5. Familiarize yourself with procedures for ensuring children only leave school with authorized adults.

6.5 Taking children out

Part of your role may well be accompanying children on school trips or outings, along with the teacher, and possibly parent volunteers. The key to successful outings is careful planning and clearly defined roles and responsibilities. It is important that responsibilities are discussed with all adults who may be involved; that there is extra support for children with special needs; that children are properly prepared for the outing; that emergency procedures are discussed and agreed; and contingency plans made in case of illness or any emergency. Keeping track of the children is vital, and there should be clear instructions as to who is responsible for each child.

> ### Points for action
>
> 1. Check the school procedures for trips and outings.
>
> 2. Make sure that you consider all aspects of each trip you are involved in that may represent potential safety hazards, and that you discuss these with the teacher.

Ensuring health and safety depends on vigilance, prompt reporting of any potential hazards and an awareness of where these may arise.

7. | CHILD ABUSE AND CHILD PROTECTION

Every teaching assistant has the duty to contribute to protecting children against abuse and neglect. School staff are ideally placed to recognize and respond to child abuse, but in some schools there remains a reluctance to get involved and a lack of certainty about what is expected on the part of many staff. For the majority of school staff, child abuse is a distressing and anxiety-provoking issue. But every year about 200 children are killed at the hands of their parents or carers and many more are injured and emotionally damaged by abuse. Sometimes the effects of abuse are lifelong. Ignoring the indicators of abuse or failing to act may consign a child to an ongoing nightmare.

No one wants to believe that the children in their care may be abused or that the parents are capable of abusing, but an acceptance that children from all walks of life suffer abuse and that all types of parents are represented among abusers is the first step in protecting children. Children may suffer from different types of abuse, including physical, emotional, sexual and neglect. Often children suffer multiple forms of abuse, and there may be more than one abuser.

There are a number of stages to the process of recognizing and responding to child abuse. These are discussed in the Area Child Protection Committee Child Protection Procedures, a copy of which is available in the school. It is important that you are aware of these procedures and that you are able to refer to them as required. They outline the responsibilities and duties of everyone involved with children to protect them from abuse and to report any concerns. LEA's also produce child protection procedures, and schools often have their own policies. Every school also has a Child Protection Liaison Teacher (CPLT) who is responsible for monitoring and supporting the child protection process within the school.

You should:

- Find and read all child protection statements and procedures within the school.

- Identify the CPLT within the school.

- Discuss the procedures with your mentor or the teacher.

7.1 Recognizing the indicators of abuse

Many adults who work with children express concern about the process of identifying the possible indicators of abuse, and the risk of confusing everyday bruises and other minor injuries with inflicted harm. There are no easy answers to give to these concerns. However, your role is not to determine whether abuse has taken place or not, but to report any concerns or suspicions you have to the appropriate person, usually the teacher or the CPLT. The indicators of abuse are many and varied, ranging from changes in children's behaviour to injuries for which the explanation seems unlikely. Your best tool within this process is your knowledge of the child and family. Sometimes children will simply tell you that abuse has taken place, in which case you need to listen carefully to the child, be calm and reassuring and then pass this information on without questioning the child further.

Indicators that may raise concerns include:

- Bruises, cuts and other injuries that do not fit the explanation given.

- Bruises on soft tissue that seem unlikely to have occurred accidentally.

- Repeated injuries, which seem unusual for the reasons given above.

- Changes in a child's behaviour, loss of ability, distress, fear or aggression.

- Persistent sexualized behaviour that is inappropriate to the child's age and understanding.

- Developmental delays, low self-esteem, poor social skills.

Many of these indicators may have non-abusive origins, including illness, stress in the family or changes in the family structure. However, a pattern of indicators, backed up by observations of the parent/child interactions and a lack of plausible alternative explanations may lead you to suspect abuse as a possible explanation.

7.2 Reporting abuse

If you have concerns about a child it is important to share these with another staff member, usually the teacher, within the boundaries of strictest confidence. The details should be given clearly and concisely, sticking to facts and avoiding opinion or speculation. The information should be discussed with the CPLT, and if your concerns are confirmed, the details will be passed to the local Social Services Department for action. Parents will normally be informed that this has been done, unless by informing them the child is put at further risk. You may be interviewed by the investigating social worker to clarify the original concerns. An investigation will take place and if the concerns are confirmed, a child protection case conference will be called. This is a multi-professional meeting, which is designed to establish the facts and the steps that must be taken to protect the child. The majority of children are not removed from their parents' care. Some children may go into the care of the local authority for a short period and then return home. A small number of children are removed permanently from home. The case conference will draw up a child protection plan, which may involve the school monitoring and supporting the child. The case conference will also place the child's name on the Child Protection Register if abuse is confirmed. The case will then be reviewed periodically to monitor progress.

Your role may include giving information to the investigation; attending the initial and review case conferences; and continuing to support the child in school. Whatever your personal feelings about the situation, it is important to remain professional and supportive in your dealings with the child's family, and to maintain confidentiality. Finally, most procedures make it clear that if your suspicions are definite enough, you should contact Social Services directly, even if the CPLT does not want to act or disagrees with you.

CONCLUSIONS

Personal and professional development is ongoing throughout our working lives, as we change and respond to new developments and demands within our job roles, or move on to new job roles. Effective development is rooted in reflective practice and responsiveness to changes within the workplace. It is important to view personal and professional development as part of the teaching assistant's role, rather than an 'extra'. Taking advantage of staff development opportunities, sharing ideas with colleagues, and discussing issues with others, are all important steps to take in developing as a reflective practitioner.

This chapter raises some of the common issues on which personal and professional development may be focused. However, each individual's job role will determine their particular development needs, and it is important to ensure that you are aware of these within your own role. Development should be based on an assessment of your existing strengths and areas for further work. This process of assessment may be formal, as part of an appraisal or development review system, or informal, through discussion with mentors or colleagues. However, it is important that it takes place as part of the ongoing process of development, which should be an integral part of your working life.

NOTES FOR FURTHER READING

Bastiani, J. (1995)
Taking a Few Risks.
London: Royal Society for the Encouragement of the Arts, Manufacture and Commerce.

Department of Health (1999)
Working Together to Safeguard Children.
London: HMSO.

Derman-Sparks, L. and the ABC Task Force (1989)
Anti-bias Curriculum Tools for Empowering Young Children.
Washington, DC: National Association for the Education of Young Children.

DES (1985)
Education for All – The Report of the Committee of Enquiry into the Education of Children from Ethnic Minority Groups chaired by Lord Swann.
London: HMSO.

DfEE (September 2000)
Teaching Assistant's File – Induction Training for Teaching Assistants.
Nottingham: DfEE.

DfEE (October 2000)
Working with Teaching Assistants – A Guide to Good Practice.
Nottingham: DfEE.

Kay, J. (2001)
Good Practice in Childcare.
London: Continuum.

Millam, R. (1996)
Anti-Discriminatory Practice – A Guide to Workers in Childcare and Education.
London: Continuum.

Milner, D. (1983)
Children and Race: Ten Years On.
London: Ward Lock Educational.

Tassoni, P. (1998)
Child Care and Education.
Oxford: Heinemann.

Woods, M. (1998)
'Early Childhood – First Principles'. Chapter 1 in Taylor, J. and Woods, M. (eds),
Early Childhood Studies – An Holistic Introduction.
London: Arnold.

CONCLUSIONS

Teaching assistants have gained a well-deserved and much needed increase in their status and role within the classroom in recent years, and proposals to extend their role further are currently in hand. Despite this, many classroom assistants are unqualified and lack access to the training they need to perform the many and diverse aspects of their role. However, the importance of training and qualifications for teaching assistants is much more clearly acknowledged now. As teachers struggle under the burden of high workloads, the need to have well-trained and qualified teaching assistants in the classroom has become crucial.

In many ways, teaching assistants have been the 'unsung heroes' of the classroom for many years, performing a wide variety of learning support and pastoral roles across their working day and week. The smooth running and good performance of many primary schools owes much to the work and commitment of their childcare assistants, classroom assistants, support workers, education care officers and all the other individuals who contribute to the effectiveness of the children's learning and social experiences in school. Teaching assistants are often very skilled, reflecting a need to develop a wide range of knowledge and expertise to meet the diverse and complex needs of many children in schools. As more children are identified with a wider range of special educational needs or learning delays, the role of the teaching assistant continues to extend to an increasing number of specialist areas.

The need for personal and professional development for teaching assistants is paramount, as their role changes and develops and offers opportunities for diversification. Developing the skills to become a reflective practitioner and analysing and seeking to meet your own development needs are very important aspects of the teaching assistant's professional role. Taking up opportunities for self-development and learning new knowledge and skills are a necessary part of this process. Teaching assistants need to build their approach to their work on a sound knowledge of children's many and diverse needs and how to meet these.

The needs of children from a wide range of backgrounds, cultures and family structures have to be understood, in the context of knowledge of anti-discriminatory practice and the impact of discrimination on children's learning development. The different ways children learn, and the range of approaches to children's learning support have to be understood to ensure children get the help that they need as individuals. Teaching assistants also need to understand and be able to respond to children with differing special educational needs, and to recognize that these vary and that each child must be treated as an individual. In addition, teaching assistants need to understand the workings of a primary school, the requirements of the National Curriculum, and how the Foundation Stage prepares children for school. How to observe and assess children, support their individual and group learning, deal with disciplinary matters and ensure that there is effective feedback for teachers from each session are all things that teaching assistants need to know. You also need to have knowledge and understanding of the goals of the literacy and numeracy strategies, what the learning objectives of Key Stage 1 Maths, English and Science are, and how these can best be met.

On top of this wide range of required knowledge, teaching assistants also need to be very skilled. Good communication skills with children and adults; teamwork skills with colleagues and parents; the ability to respond to children's emotional needs and to express appropriate warmth and regard for them; and the skills to manage busy and diverse workloads are only some of the requirements of the teaching assistant in your day-to-day work. You also need to have patience, motivation, sensitivity, tact and a good sense of humour to deal with the many problems or issues which are part of the daily life of a primary school.

The role of the teaching assistant is challenging in both the range and depth of what is expected both in and outside the classroom. Teaching assistants need to have the opportunity and motivation to build their knowledge and understanding and develop their skills. For some of you this will mean attendance on specific training courses or qualification courses, such as the CACHE Specialist Teaching Assistants Award, or LEA induction and training courses for teaching assistants. Some of you may already have qualifications and others may follow a programme to complete an NVQ for Classroom/Teaching Assistants. Whatever your approach is to building and extending your knowledge and skills it is important to seek support within the school from teachers and other colleagues, and to ensure that your development needs are analysed and met within the resources available. Hopefully, this handbook will have provided you with some of the underpinning knowledge and understanding to start this process and to support you on courses such as the CACHE Specialist Teaching Assistants Award. Good luck!

APPENDIX

CHAPTER 2, EXERCISE 2.1

1. Davey is learning, by exploring, about the properties of the materials he is using and gaining knowledge of how they behave when he manipulates them. This part of play, gaining new knowledge through exploration, is an important part of learning. However, Davey would benefit from adult support to take his explorations further, perhaps using a wider range of materials and different types of paint, and through talking about his 'experiments'. The social aspects of learning are also important.

2. It is possible that the children are not learning much from this experience, as they contribute very little to the finished product and they have few choices in the process. It is important to remember that learning takes place in the process and not in the product. The children would benefit more from discussing and looking at different shapes, choosing materials and then drawing and cutting out their own shape, and then choosing how (and if) they want to decorate their shapes from a wide range of materials.

3. This activity provides the children with a social experience of learning and gives them choice in their planning and making of the model. It is important, however, to ensure that less confident children get support to contribute and that the activity is 'scaffolded' as required, for individual children.

CHAPTER 3, EXERCISE 3.2

1. Sitting with Anna during whole class teaching, both to encourage and prompt her to participate, and to observe her levels of understanding. Working with Anna during individual and small group work, to support her learning, through checking her understanding of the task, working with her to achieve the task, and talking to her about her work. Anna might benefit from differentiated work, which includes more structured play activities, perhaps with a small group of other children who have similar needs. It would be helpful to find out about Anna's previous learning in order to build on that through planned activities.

2. Making a good relationship with Anna is a key to helping her, sharing ideas and listening to her, giving genuine praise and encouragement. Good communication skills, tact and sensitivity are important. Anna should be made to feel important and special because of the extra attention, not stigmatized. Good use of observation and questioning skills are also important.

CHAPTER 3, EXERCISE 3.3

Factors that could promote good listening skills:

- Encouraging turn-taking in speaking and listening.

- Modelling good listening skills.

- Using non-verbal skills to indicate listening e.g. facial expressions, body posture.

- Promoting a quiet and orderly environment.

- Paraphrasing (repeating back) what a child has said to check other children's understanding.

- Praising and encouraging children who listen well.

- Ensuring children who have communication difficulties or who have English as a second language have a chance to speak and are listened to.

- Valuing and respecting everyone's contribution.

Factors that could inhibit good listening skills:

- Noise, disorder and lack of structure.

- Busy, rushed adults who do not listen themselves.

- Lack of time for speaking and listening.

- Failure to encourage quiet or shy children.

- Allowing certain children to dominate.

- Letting children all speak at once.

- Valuing some contributions more than others.

Teaching assistant's contribution could be:

- Listening carefully to children without interrupting.

- Encouraging quiet children to speak.

- Encouraging good behaviour and turn-taking in speaking.

- Commenting on what you have heard in a positive way, to indicate you have listened.

- Inviting other children to comment on what has been said.

- Promoting a quiet and orderly environment.

- Promoting respect between all individuals.

CHAPTER 3, EXERCISE 3.6

1. You could suggest that it is Yellow table's turn for help today, and that other groups will get help at other times. You could mention that you are interested in what the children have to contribute to the topic. You could ask if it is OK for you to join in with them. A relaxed and supportive approach is important, rather than 'taking over' the task and dominating the process.

2. Making suggestion as required, for example, commenting on positive characteristics you have noticed about a child, if they are stuck trying to describe themselves. Discussing how the drawings might be done. Helping the children to write by scribing for them, helping with spellings if a child gets stuck, praising the children's efforts if they write independently. It is also helpful to talk through the children's ideas so that they are prepared to contribute to the whole class discussion. You can then prompt the child who may forget what he/she wants to say. In terms of whole class comparisons, you could draw out comparisons within the group e.g. differences in height, eye colour and personality to illustrate what 'compare' means.

3. The task could be differentiated by using oral discussion more than written work within the group, so that the children feedback to the class verbally. This may support children who do not draw or write particularly well and who may not gain from their work being shown to the class.

4. Through ensuring that the children understand the key concepts such as 'characteristics' and 'compare', by discussing these concepts and giving examples. You need to ensure that the children recognize that they are all valued for their uniqueness and their own special contributions. You should also be careful to make sure that those children who give more oral and fewer written contributions are equally praised for their work.

CHAPTER 4, EXERCISE 4.1

- Collecting money.
- Lining up.
- Science activities.
- Cooking.
- Singing, dancing and music.
- General conversation with children.
- PE.
- Taking the register.
- Working with individual children.
- Literacy hour.

CHAPTER 6, EXERCISE 6.1

- A teacher noting that a child's writing development is well advanced compared to the rest of the classes.

- The work could be differentiated to extend the child, by adding on additional tasks. The child could be asked to write more about a subject, or to answer more questions or look at additional aspects.

- A teaching assistant reporting verbally to the teacher that a group she had been working with found the set activity confusing and too hard.

- The teaching assistant could differentiate tasks for this group in future, learning through observation and discussion, where their starting point is for new learning. The teaching assistant could discuss the learning objectives with the teacher and develop new approaches that would be more helpful for these children. The children may need some special sessions, going back to cover earlier stages of work again, to strengthen their prior experiences before tackling the new learning.

- A parent volunteer commenting to the teacher that a child who had some behavioural problems in school worked quietly and with concentration during drawing and painting activities.

- The child's skill in this area should be acknowledged and discussed, with the child, parents and teacher. The child should be encouraged to represent her ideas through drawing and painting, and to share these ideas with others. The parent volunteer could be asked to continue working with this child, developing good communication and speaking skills.

- A teaching assistant working with an individual child reports that the child has become unhappy about leaving the class to do one-to-one work during parts of her literacy hour.

- The child may be feeling stigmatized by leaving the class. She may feel ready to do more work in the class. The teaching assistant could work with the child within the class, or work with her group, supporting several children to reduce the stigma of being supported individually. The teaching assistant could work with the child in a pair or small group outside the class, or any combination of the above.

CHAPTER 7, EXERCISE 7.2

Chris and Harry

1. Talk to Chris about how Harry may be feeling and what it may be like to be left out of games and playtime talk. Ask Chris if he could befriend Harry and help him back into friendship groups, by inviting him to play and including him in activities sometimes.

Explain to Harry that Chris feels that he takes over, and that it is important to share and support each other in games. Ask some of the other children to befriend Harry at break and lunchtime so he does not always play with Harry. Explain that it is not OK to continue to fight and shout, and that other children are getting upset.

2. Avoid focusing exclusively on the two children. Consider ways in which the whole class can develop listening skills, respect and empathy for each other. Use stories and role play about resolving conflict to help the children understand the issues.

CHAPTER 7, EXERCISE 7.3

- **During 'carpet time' Ryan ties his shoelace to that of the child next to him, creating a domino effect so that after twenty minutes four children are shackled together.**

- Quietly lean over and ask Ryan to untie the laces. Then ask the next child and so on. After the session, speak to Ryan quietly, suggesting that the shoelace incident was disruptive to the class and might have been dangerous when the children got up. Be firm that it should not happen again and remind Ryan how he should behave on the carpet.

- **During whole class teaching in literacy hour, Hannah leans forward and starts to twiddle with the hair of the child in front of her, distracting about five other children in the process.**

- Without disrupting the session, lean over Hannah and quietly ask her to stop twiddling. Remind her and the other children to pay attention to the teacher. Sit close to Hannah in case there is any repetition.

- **During silent reading, several boys gather at the shelves to 'change their books', and instead start to chat among themselves about toys.**

- Suggest to the boys that they are having a really nice conversation, which they should continue at break, but now they need to choose books and go back to their seats. Stay with them and make sure they choose books as quickly as possible, helping them if necessary.

- **Kay and David reach for the same pencil at their table and then start a loud squabble about who should have it, culminating in pushing and shoving each other off their chairs.**

- In a firm but quiet voice tell them both to sit down and then make sure they both have a pencil. Remind the other children to get on with their work. Speak briefly to the two children at break to make sure the row will not rumble on into the playground.

- **At dinnertime, Dan leaps out of the queue for lunches and entertains the other children by dancing round, pulling faces and blowing 'raspberries', until the queue collapses.**

- Return Dan to his place in the queue and stay with him until he has settled down. Explain that it takes longer to get lunches out if children do not co-operate and this might mean that some children will not have enough time to play. Ask Dan to help with ensuring that all the children have a good lunchtime, by staying quietly in the queue. In a firm voice, ask the other children to line up again. Repeat this request if necessary.

- **Karen and Shiraz, both seven, rampage around the playground play-fighting with each other, shouting at the top of their voices, oblivious of others until they flatten a smaller child.**

- Check that the young child is unhurt. Take the two children aside and explain that although we want them to have fun, they need to be careful that no one gets hurt. Remind them of any relevant school rules. Ask them to make sure that the smaller child is OK for the rest of the break.

- **Supposedly absorbed in completing drawings of different types of dwelling places, Mark entertains his table by drawing pictures of 'willies'.**

- Provide Mark with a fresh piece of paper and ask him to get on with the task. Sit with him and help him to get started. Make sure he knows what he is supposed to be doing and how to tackle the task. If he tries to talk about his behaviour, respond briefly and show little interest, explaining gently but firmly that this is not what was required. Do not show any shock or outrage, or tell him off. Disinterest is a much better way of dealing with this behaviour.

  One note of caution – taken with other behavioural indicators and in the context of the family and environment, there is a small possibility that such drawings could be linked to sexual abuse. Mention the incident to the teacher and monitor future behaviour.

- **Cheryl asks Tom to pass her a rubber, instead he throws, she catches and tosses it back and so on.**

- Catch the rubber and remove it from play. Remind the children to get on with their work and stay in the vicinity for a while until they settle.

- **Harry refers to the child next to him as 'you prat'.**

- Immediately, but without raising your voice, tell Harry that this is not acceptable behaviour. At break ask Harry to consider how his comment may have hurt the child's feelings and ask him to apologize. If there is repetition, suggest to the teacher that some whole class work on support and respect for each other may be needed.

- **Fauzia and Jane follow the lunchtime supervisor down the playground doing an exaggerated imitation of her walk.**

- Very firmly tell them to stop. Take the children aside and firmly, but quietly, tell them that this behaviour is not acceptable. Remind them that lunchtime supervisors are there to support and help them and that they should not be treated disrespectfully. Organize a job for the children, which will help the lunchtime supervisor, such as making sure smaller children are OK, for the rest of the break.

CHAPTER 7, EXERCISE 7.4

Beth may benefit from working outside the class for a period of time, in order to help her overcome her concerns about writing, without the pressure of being in 'public', and because she may hear better in a quieter place. It may be helpful to do some more work on phonics with Beth, using audio tapes to help her hear sounds and then write them down. Scribing for Beth in the first few sessions may help her build confidence. Using alliterative rhymes and poems may also help. It may also be easier to manage her behaviour away from the class by getting her to concentrate for increasingly long periods of time. Build her confidence through praise and encouragement. Involve her parents and encourage them to read poems and rhymes with her, and to play games such as 'I Spy'.

CHAPTER 8, EXERCISE 8.3

This incident may be best dealt with at whole class level, as often the use of a particular term becomes rife in a group of children. Dealing with a single child is not necessarily going to stop this type of incident happening. Trying to get to the bottom of who introduced the word is pointless. The teacher needs to remind the whole class that calling other children names hurts, is unkind, and is not acceptable in school. The teacher may also want to encourage the children to discuss what different terms mean and how they are offensive, or to remind the children that they must not use terms they do not understand.

Gavin may need extra support and monitoring because there may be underlying reasons why he is a target for abuse. The boys who called him names should be asked to apologize, and any other signs of bullying should be brought to the attention of the teacher.

GLOSSARY

Anti-discriminatory Practice – an approach to practice, which acknowledges the discrimination experienced by some individuals and groups and actively seeks to redress the negative impact of this.

Area Child Protection Committee Child Protection Procedures – guidelines for all practitioners working with children on their responsibilities towards protecting those children from abuse and neglect.

Bachelor of Education (B.Ed.) – teaching qualification of either three or four years' duration

BTEC/EdExcel – national awarding body for a range of qualifications including childcare and education e.g. BTEC National Diploma in Early Childhood.

CACHE (the Council for Awards in Children's Care and Education) – national awarding body for qualifications in the early years.

CACHE Diploma – nursery nurse qualification awarded by the Council for Awards in Children's Care and Education.

CACHE Specialist Teaching Assistant Award – one-year course to train teaching assistants, focusing on supporting teachers in the classroom and core National Curriculum subjects at KS1 CACHE.

Cardinal number – the last number in counting a set of objects, which names the set and indicates the size of the set.

Child Protection Liaison Teacher (CPLT) – a teacher designated to deal with child protection issues in school.

Child Protection Register – a list of children who have been abused held by a child protection agency in each local authority.

Code of Practice for Special Educational Needs – regulations for identifying and supporting children with learning difficulties or delays or emotional or behavioural problems that affect their learning.

Culture – the sorts of customs and practices, beliefs and ideas of a particular group in society.

Curriculum Guidance for the Foundation Stage (QCA, 2000) – document supporting teaching and learning in the Foundation Stage for 3 to 5-year-olds, providing curriculum guidance for educare providers working towards the Early Learning Goals.

Differentiation – in this context, the process by which the content and sometimes the teaching objectives of a planned session are varied to meet the needs of children of different ability or at different stages of development.

Educational psychologists – employed by the LEA to assess children's special educational needs and suggest strategies to support the child in school.

Foundation Stage – children aged 3–5 working towards the Early Learning Goals.

Individual Education Plan (IEP) – school targets and learning objectives for children with SEN, set and reviewed regularly by the teacher, parents and SENCO and other relevant professionals at a regular review meeting.

Information and communications technology (ICT) – National Curriculum subject involving the development of skills in using computer technology and the internet.

Key Stage 1 (KS1) – first phase of the National Curriculum for children aged 5–7.

Local Education Authority (LEA) – the local government body responsible for the provision of education within the authority, including support for schools.

Makaton – sign language specifically developed to support children and adults with learning difficulties.

Multi-lingual and Bilingual Children – children who communicate in more than one language and who may not have English as a first language.

National Childcare Strategy – introduced by the government in 1998 to improve quality and standards in childcare and to promote the growth of childcare places.

National Literacy Strategy – introduced by the Department for Education and Employment in 1998 to provide a framework for teaching and learning literacy.

National Numeracy Strategy – introduced in 1999 by the Department for Education and Employment to provide a framework for teaching and learning maths.

NNEB – nursery nurse qualification, replaced by CACHE Diploma.

NVQ's for Teaching/Classroom Assistants – competence based qualifications at Level 2 and 3 offering teaching assistants vocational qualifications specifically tailored to their job role (www.lgnto.org.uk).

Onset-rime – onset is the first sound in a word, rime is the part from the vowel onwards e.g. c-at, sl-ip.

Phonemes – there are about forty-four phonemes (different sounds) in the English language.

Phonological awareness – the ability to understand the different sounds within words and to manipulate them.

Physiotherapists and occupational therapists – normally employed by the Health Authority to support children's physical development, co-ordination, balance and mobility.

Post-graduate Certificate in Education – teaching qualification, usually one-year full-time study for graduates with degrees in a curriculum subject or Early Childhood Studies.

Programme of Study (PoS) – part of the National Curriculum guidance for each subject to help teachers plan their delivery.

Social workers – employed by the Local Authority Social Services Department to work with children at risk and in need and their families.

Special educational needs (SEN) – children who need additional help and support to learn due to emotional, behavioural and/or learning delays or difficulties.

Special Educational Needs Co-ordinator (SENCO) – the teacher designated to co-ordinate school support for children with SEN in school and to liaise with parents and professionals from other agencies.

Speech therapists – employed by the local Health Authority to support children with speech impairments and language delays.

Standard Assessment Tests – national assessment tests for children at the end of Key Stages 1, 2 and 3, which are used to judge children's progress and evaluate the effectiveness of individual schools.

Statutory Attainment Targets (SATs) – targets against which teachers can judge children's progress in each National Curriculum subject area.

Subitizing – the ability to recognize the cardinal number of a small number of objects without counting them individually.

Zone of proximal development (ZPD) – a central theme in Vygotsky's social constructivist theory of how children learn. The ZPD is the stage of development which a child is entering next.

INDEX